Step-by-step Recipes and Essential Cooking Techniques:

Tips, and Tricks for Easy Cooking

Stanley B. Molloy

Contents

PUDDINGS

VEGETABLES

SOUPS

BREAD AND CAKES

Jellies and Creams

Soufflées and Omelets

Invalid Cookery

Supper Dishes and Salads

Miscellaneous Dishes

Odds and Ends

How to use up Fragments

Forcemeats

Preserves

Orange Pudding.

Ingredients—The rind and juice of 2 oranges.
2 oz. of cake-crumbs rubbed through a sieve.
2 oz. of castor sugar.
3 eggs.
1 gill of milk or cream.

Method.—Put the crumbs in a basin, with the sugar.
Add the grated rind of one orange, and the juice of the two.
Beat in the yolks of the three eggs, and add the milk or cream.
Whip the white of one egg to a stiff froth, stir in lightly.
Line a pie-dish with a little good pastry; pour the mixture in.
Bake until set, and of a light brown colour.

Welcome-Guest Pudding.

Ingredients—¼ lb. of suet.
¼ lb. of sugar.
¼ lb. of cake-crumbs, or ratafias, rubbed through a sieve.
¼ lb. of bread-crumbs.
The rind and juice of one lemon.
3 eggs, well beaten.

Method.—Put all the dry ingredients into a basin.
Add the lemon rind and juice, and mix with the eggs.
Put into a well-greased mould.
Cover with buttered paper, and steam for two hours.

Crème Frite.

Ingredients—1 whole egg.

1 white.

4 yolks.

1 gill of cream.

1 gill of milk.

1 tablespoonful of castor sugar.

Flavouring to taste.

3 oz. of cake-crumbs.

Method.—Cream the yolks and white well together with the castor sugar.

Add cream, milk, and flavouring.

Strain this custard into a greased pudding-basin, and steam *very gently*, until firm.

Let it get quite cold; then turn it out.

Cut into slices about one-third of an inch thick.

Stamp into round or fancy shapes.

Egg and cake-crumb them.

Fry in a frying-basket in hot fat.

Serve on a glass dish, and sprinkle with castor sugar.

Gâteau de Cerise.

Ingredients—1 lb. of cooking cherries.

¼ lb. of lump sugar.

½ pint of water.

A few drops of cochineal.

¾ of an ounce-packet of gelatine.

The juice of one lemon.

Method.—Boil the sugar and water; add the lemon and skim well.

Add the cherries (stoned), and stew for a quarter of an hour.

Melt the gelatine in a little water, and add it to the cherries, with enough cochineal to colour brightly.

Pour the mixture into a border mould.

When set, dip it in hot water for a second or two, and turn on to a glass dish.

Serve with whipped cream in the centre.

Jaune Mange.

Ingredients—½ ounce packet of gelatine.

½ pint of water.

½ pint of white wine.

Juice of one and a half lemon.

Rind of half a lemon.

3 oz. of castor sugar.

4 yolks.

Method.—Soak the gelatine in the water with the lemon rind.

Then put it in a saucepan with all the other ingredients.

Stir over the fire until the custard thickens; but, on no account, let it boil.

Then strain into a wetted mould.

Apple Charlotte.

Ingredients—2 lb. of apples.

½ lb. of moist sugar.

Grated rind of a lemon.

Slices of broad.

Some clarified butter.

Method.—Peel and core the apples, and stew them with the sugar, lemon rind, and a quarter pint of water, until reduced to half the quantity.

Take a plain round tin, holding about a pint and a half.

Cut a round of stale bread, about one-eighth of an inch thick; dip it in clarified butter, and lay it in the bottom of the mould.

Line the sides with slices of bread, cut about an inch wide, and one-eighth of an inch thick, and also dipped in butter.

Pour the apple mixture into the mould.

Cover with another round of bread dipped in butter; and bake in a moderately quick oven for three quarters of an hour.

For serving, turn it on to a hot dish, and sprinkle castor sugar over it.

Viennoise Pudding.

Ingredients—5 oz. of stale crumb of bread cut into dice.

3 oz. of sultanas.

¼ lb. of castor sugar.

2 oz. of candied peel.

Grated rind of a lemon.

1 wineglass of sherry.

½ pint of milk.

2 whole eggs.

1 oz. of lump sugar.

Method.—Put the 1 oz. of lump sugar into an old saucepan, and burn it a dark brown.

Pour in the milk, and stir until it is well coloured and the sugar dissolved.

Beat the eggs well, strain the coloured milk on to them, and add the sherry.

Put all the dry ingredients into a basin, and pour the eggs, milk, and sherry over them.

Let the pudding soak for half an hour.

Then put it into a well-greased pint-mould.

Cover with buttered paper, and steam for one hour and a half.

This pudding is to be served with German sauce (*see* Sauces).

Snow Pudding.

Ingredients—½ pint of milk.

1½ oz. of bread-crumbs.

Grated rind of a lemon.

2 tablespoonfuls of caster sugar.

3 eggs.

2 tablespoonfuls of strawberry or any other jam.

A little pastry.

Method.—Put the bread-crumbs into a basin.

Boil the milk, and pour it over them.

Mix in the sugar, one whole egg, and two yolks well beaten, and add the lemon rind.

Line a pint pie-dish with a little pastry.

Spread the jam at the bottom and pour the mixture over.

Bake in a moderate oven until set.

Beat the remaining whites to a stiff froth, with a dessertspoonful of castor sugar; and heap it lightly on the top just before serving.

German Puffs.

Ingredients—2 eggs.

Their weight in castor sugar, and ground rice.

The grated rind of a lemon.

Method.—Beat the eggs well.

Then stir in, gradually, the castor sugar and ground rice, and add the lemon rind.

Partly fill well-buttered cups, or moulds, with the mixture; and bake in a moderate oven for a quarter of an hour, or twenty minutes.

Serve with a wine or sweet sauce (*see* Sauces).

Apple Amber Pudding.

Ingredients—8 apples.

2½ oz. of butter.

3 oz. of moist sugar.

Rind and juice of one lemon.

3 eggs.

A little pastry.

Method.—Wash the apples (they need not be peeled or cored) and cut them into small pieces.

Put them into a stewpan with the butter, sugar, lemon rind and juice, and stew until tender.

Then rub through a hair sieve—the sieve keeps back the peel and pips.

Beat the three yolks into the mixture, and put it into a pint pie-dish lined with a little pastry.

Bake in a moderate oven until set.

Then beat the whites of the eggs to a stiff froth with a dessertspoonful of castor sugar, and heap on the top.

Put it, again, into a cool oven, until the whites are set.

This pudding may be served either hot or cold.

Apple Pudding.

Ingredients—1 lb. of flour.

6 or 8 oz. of suet.

A pinch of salt.

1 teaspoonful of baking powder.

Some apples.

3 tablespoonfuls or more of moist sugar.

The grated rind of a small lemon.

2 or 3 cloves.

Method.—Prepare the paste, and line a basin as for beef-steak pudding.

Put in the apples, which should be pared and cored, and sprinkle in the sugar and lemon rind.

Put on the cover of paste, and tie over it a well-scalded and floured cloth.

Boil for one hour, or longer: the length of time will depend on the fruit used.

Any fresh fruit may be substituted for the apple.

Raspberry Pudding.

Ingredients—1 pint of raspberries.

3 oz. of sugar.

Thin slices of bread.

A little milk.

Method.—Pick the stalks from the raspberries, and mix them with the sugar.

Put them and the bread in alternate layers in a pie-dish, moistening the bread with a little milk.

Bake for half an hour.

Note.—This pudding is very good served with cream or custards. The bottled raspberries may be used instead of fresh fruit.

Lemon Pudding.

Ingredients—½ lb. of bread-crumbs.

¼ lb. of finely-chopped suet.

¼ lb. of castor sugar.

The grated rind of one lemon, and the juice of two.

2 eggs.

Enough milk to mix it.

Method.—Put the bread-crumbs and suet into a basin.

Add sugar, grated lemon-rind, and juice.

Mix the pudding with the two eggs, well beaten, and a very little milk.

Boil it for one hour and a half.

This pudding may be served with a wine or sweet sauce (*see* Sauces).

Marmalade Pudding.

Ingredients—½ lb. of flour.

½ lb. of bread-crumbs.

½ lb. of finely-chopped suet.

½ lb. of moist sugar.

½ lb. of marmalade.

2 eggs.

The grated rind of a lemon.

Method.—Put the flour, bread-crumbs, suet, sugar, and lemon rind into a basin.

Mix with the marmalade and two eggs, well beaten, and, if necessary, a little milk.

Put it into a well-greased pudding-basin, and tie over it a scalded and floured cloth.

Boil it for five hours.

General Satisfaction.

Ingredients—3 sponge cakes.

2 tablespoonfuls of strawberry or other jam.

1 wineglass of sherry.

Rather more than ½ a pint of milk.

4 eggs.

1 tablespoonful of sugar.

A little pastry.

Method.—Line a pie-dish with a little pastry.

Spread the jam at the bottom, and lay on it the sponge cakes, cut in halves.

Beat one whole egg and three yolks well together.

Mix with the sugar and milk, and pour over the sponge cakes.

Bake in a moderate oven until the custard is set.

Beat the three whites stiffly, and lay on the top of the pudding.

Put into a cool oven until the whites are set, and of a pale fawn colour.

This pudding may be served hot or cold.

Marlborough Pudding.

Ingredients—1 pint of milk.

2 tablespoonfuls of flour.

2 whole eggs and 2 yolks.

The grated rind of a lemon.

3 oz. of castor sugar.

2 oz. of butter.

Method.—Mix the flour smoothly with the milk, and stir over the fire until it boils and thickens.

Add the sugar, the eggs, well beaten, the grated lemon rind, and the butter beaten to a cream.

Line a pie-dish with pastry; pour in the mixture.

Bake in a moderate oven until set.

Yorkshire (or Batter) Pudding.

Ingredients—½ lb. of flour.

1 pint of milk.

2 eggs.

A pinch of salt.

Method.—Put the flour into a basin, make a hole in the middle, and put in the eggs unbeaten.

Stir smoothly round with a wooden spoon, adding the milk very gradually.

If it is to be served with meat, bake it in a baking-tin, which should be well greased with quite one ounce of butter or clarified dripping.

Curate's Puddings.

Ingredients—The weight of 3 eggs in each sugar, flour, and butter.

4 eggs.

A little flavouring essence of any kind, or the grated rind of a lemon.

Method.—Rub the butter well into the flour.

Add the sugar and the four eggs, well beaten.

Half fill well-buttered cups or moulds, and bake for twenty minutes or half an hour.

Serve with a wine or sweet sauce (*see* Sauces).

Canary Pudding.

Ingredients—2 tablespoonfuls of flour.

2 tablespoonfuls of sugar

1 pint of milk.

2 eggs.

Method.—Put the milk and sugar on to boil.

Mix the flour with a little cold milk.

When the milk boils pour in the flour, and stir it briskly until it thickens.

When cool, add the two eggs, well beaten.

Bake in a greased pie-dish for half an hour.

Christmas Pudding.

Ingredients—2 lb. of raisins.

1 lb. of suet.

½ lb. of candied peel.

¾ lb. of flour.

¼ lb. of bread-crumbs,

¼ lb. of moist sugar.

A little mixed spice.

Half a nutmeg grated.

A little lemon rind grated.

½ pint of milk.

4 eggs.

Method.—Put the dry ingredients into a basin, and mix with the eggs, well beaten, and the milk.

Put into a well-greased basin, and boil ten hours if possible.

Cabinet Pudding.

Ingredients—A few raisins or cherries.

1 dozen sponge finger-biscuits.

1 oz. of castor sugar.

1 pint of milk.

2 whole eggs and 2 yolks.

A little vanilla or other flavouring.

Method.—Decorate a well-buttered pint-and-a-half mould with raisins or preserved cherries.

Beat the eggs and milk well together.

Sweeten with the sugar, and add the flavouring.

Break the cakes into pieces.

Put a quarter of them at the bottom of the mould.

Pour in a little of the custard, then more pieces of cake and more custard, and continue in this way until the mould is full.

Cover with buttered paper, and steam gently for about an hour.

Auntie's Pudding.

Ingredients—½ lb. of flour.

¼ lb. of finely-chopped suet.

¼ lb. of currants, well washed and dried.

3 oz. of sugar.

1 egg.

A little milk.

Method.—Put all the dry ingredients into a basin.

Mix with the egg, well beaten, and the milk.

Boil in a well-greased basin for an hour and a quarter.

Rhubarb Fool.

Ingredients—14 sticks of rhubarb.

½ lb. of moist sugar (more, if necessary).

½ pint of water.

1 gill of milk.

The thin rind of half a lemon.

Method.—Cut the rhubarb in small pieces.

Stew gently with the sugar and water until quite tender.

Rub through a sieve.

Add the milk, and serve cold.

Scrap Pudding.

Ingredients—Some scraps of bread.

¼ lb. of moist sugar.

¼ lb. of finely-chopped suet.

The grated rind of a lemon.

2 eggs, well beaten.

¾ pint of milk.

Some preserve.

Method.—Dry the bread in a slow oven until it is hard.

Pound it in a mortar, and measure 6 ounces of the powder; mix it with the suet and sugar.

Add the lemon rind; pour over the milk, and add the eggs.

Beat well for a few minutes.

Then put the mixture in layers in a pie-dish alternately with the preserve.

Let the top layer be the pudding mixture.

Bake in a moderate oven until the mixture is set.

Bread-and-Cheese Pudding.

Ingredients—6 oz. of dried and powdered bread.

½ lb. of grated cheese.

½ pint of milk.

1 egg, well beaten.

Pepper and salt.

A little cayenne.

Method.—Mix all the ingredients together, and bake in a pie-dish until the mixture is set.

Mould of Rice.

Ingredients—½ lb. of rice.

1 quart of milk.

¼ lb. of moist or castor sugar.

Method.—Boil the rice with the sugar in the milk until it is perfectly soft.

Then put it into a mould.

When cold, turn it out, and serve it with jam.

Norfolk Dumpling.

Ingredients—Some bread dough.

Method.—Make the dough into small round balls.

Drop them into fast-boiling water, and boil quickly for twenty minutes.

Serve immediately, either with meat or with sweet sauce.

Sago Pudding.

Ingredients—1 pint of milk.

2 tablespoonfuls of sago.

2 tablespoonfuls of sugar.

1 egg.

Method.—Simmer the sago in the milk until it thickens.

Add the sugar and the egg, well beaten.

Put it into a pie-dish, and bake in a moderate oven for half an hour.

The egg may be omitted if preferred.

Rice Pudding.

Ingredients—1 pint of milk.

2 tablespoonfuls of rice.

2 tablespoonfuls of sugar.

Method.—Wash the rice and put it in a pie-dish with the sugar.

Pour the milk over it and let it soak for an hour.

Then bake in a moderate oven for one hour, or more, until the rice is quite cooked.

If eggs are used the rice must be simmered in the milk before they are added, and then poured into the pie-dish.

Tapioca Pudding.

Make like a rice pudding.

Semolina Pudding.

Ingredients—1 pint of milk.

2 tablespoonfuls of semolina.

1 tablespoonful of moist sugar.

An egg, if liked.

Method.—Simmer the semolina in the milk, with the sugar, stirring until it thickens.

Then beat in the egg.

Put in a pie-dish, and bake for half an hour.

Swiss Apple Pudding.

Ingredients—½ lb. of bread-crumbs.

3 oz. of suet, finely chopped.

¼ lb. of apples, finely minced.

¼ lb. of sugar.

The juice and grated rind of one lemon.

1 egg well beaten.

Method.—Mix all the ingredients well together, and bake in a pie-dish for one hour.

Light Sultana Pudding.

Ingredients—3 eggs.

Their weight in each—butter, flour, and sugar.

¼ lb. of sultanas.

The grated rind of a lemon.

Method.—Beat the butter to a cream.

Mix in gradually the flour and sugar, alternately with the eggs, which should be well beaten.

Then add the sultanas, well cleaned, and the grated lemon rind.

Steam for three hours.

Fun Pudding.

Ingredients—1 lb. of apples.

2 tablespoonfuls of apricot jam.

2 tablespoonfuls of sugar.

1 oz. of butter.

2 dessertspoonfuls of arrowroot.

1 pint of milk.

Method.—Peel and core the apples, and slice them very finely.

Lay them at the bottom of a pie-dish, and sprinkle some sugar over them.

Put the butter about them in little pieces, and spread over the apricot jam.

Boil the milk, with the remainder of the sugar, and then stir it into the arrowroot, mixed smoothly with cold milk.

When it thickens, pour over the apricot and apples, and bake for half an hour.

Sweet Custard Pudding.

Ingredients—Some apricot jam.

3 eggs.

1 pint of hot milk.

3 tablespoonfuls of castor or moist sugar.

The grated rind of a lemon.

A little pastry.

Method.—Line a pie-dish neatly with the pastry, and spread the jam at the bottom.

Beat the eggs with the milk and sugar, and pour over the jam.

Bake in a very moderate oven for about one hour.

Jam Roly-poly Pudding.

Ingredients—1 lb. of flour.

4, 6, or 8 oz. of suet, finely chopped.

Some red jam.

1 teaspoonful of baking powder.

Method.—Put the flour into a basin, and add to it the suet and baking powder.

Mix it with a little cold water and roll it out.

Spread it with the jam, and roll up in the form of a bolster.

Scald and flour a cloth, and sew, or tie, the pudding firmly in it.

Boil for two hours.

Treacle Roly-poly Pudding.

Make like a jam roly-poly, using treacle instead of jam.

Custard Pudding.

Ingredients—1 pint of hot milk.

3 eggs.

2 tablespoonfuls of castor sugar.

A little flavouring essence.

A little pastry.

Method.—Line a pie-dish with pastry.

Beat the eggs in the milk, with the sugar.

Add the flavouring essence, and strain into the pie-dish.

Bake in a moderate oven for one hour, or until set.

NOTE.—A richer custard may be made by using five yolks and one whole egg.

Bread-and-Butter Pudding.

Ingredients—Some slices of bread-and-butter.

2 tablespoonfuls of sugar.

1 pint of milk.

A few currants, nicely washed.

1 or 2 eggs, if liked.

Method.—Put some thin slices of bread-and-butter in the bottom of a pie-dish.

Sprinkle them with sugar and currants.

Lay some more slices on the top, with more sugar and currants.

Pour over the milk, and let it soak for half an hour.

Then bake until set.

If eggs are used, beat them with the milk.

Ginger Pudding.

Ingredients—8 oz. of bread-crumbs.

6 oz. of suet, finely chopped.

½ lb. of treacle.

2 tablespoonfuls of moist sugar.

2 teaspoonfuls of ground ginger.

2 oz. of flour.

1 teaspoonful of baking powder.

Method.—Put the bread-crumbs, suet, flour, ginger, and baking powder into a basin.

Mix with the treacle.

Boil in a basin, or cloth, for two hours.

Fig Pudding.

Ingredients—½ lb. of bread-crumbs.

¼ lb. of suet, finely chopped.

3 oz. of brown sugar.

2 oz. of flour.

The grated rind of a lemon.

1 egg.

½ lb. of figs.

A little milk.

Method.—Put the bread-crumbs, suet, and sugar, with the figs, cut small, into a basin.

Add the flour and lemon rind, and mix with the egg, well beaten, and a little milk.

Boil in a well-greased basin for two hours.

Rice Balls.

Ingredients—½ lb. of rice.

1 quart of milk or water.

3 tablespoonfuls of moist sugar.

Method.—Wash the rice well.

Put it with the sugar and milk, or water, into a large saucepan.

Boil gently for about one hour.

Then press into cups, and turn on to a dish.

These may be served with jam, treacle, butter and sugar, or with a sweet sauce.

Little Batter Puddings.

Ingredients—¼ lb. of flour.

½ pint of milk.

1 egg.

Some jam.

Method.—Put the flour into a bowl, and make a well in the middle.

Put in the egg, mix smoothly with a wooden spoon, adding the milk by degrees.

Grease some little patty-pans, and half fill them with the batter.

Bake in a quick oven.

When done, dish on a folded napkin, and put a little jam on each.

Ellen's Pudding.

Ingredients—A little pastry.

1 oz. of butter.

2 oz. of sugar.

½ pint of milk.

The grated rind of a lemon.

1 egg well beaten.

2 oz. of cake-crumbs.

Method.—Beat the butter to a cream in a basin.

Mix in the sugar thoroughly.

Add the milk gradually.

Then add the egg and cake-crumbs, and pour the mixture into a pie-dish lined with a little pastry.

It is an improvement to put some jam at the bottom of the dish.

Bake for about half an hour.

Bread-and-Fruit Pudding.

Ingredients—Slices of stale bread.

1 pint of raspberries.

½ pint of currants.

¼ lb. of sugar.

Method.—Line a cake-tin, or pie-dish, with stale bread, cut to fit it nicely.

Stew the fruit with the sugar until nicely cooked.

Pour into the mould, and cover with slices of bread.

Cover it with a plate, with a weight on it, and let it stand until the next day.

Turn it out and serve plain, or with custard, whipped cream, or milk thickened with cornflour (*see* Cheap Custard).

Ground-Rice Pudding.

Ingredients—2 tablespoonfuls of ground rice.

1 pint of milk.

2 oz. of sugar.

1 or 2 eggs (these may be omitted if liked).

A little grated lemon rind, or flavouring essence.

Method.—Boil the milk with the sugar.

Mix the rice smoothly with a little cold milk.

Pour it into the boiling milk, and stir until it thickens.

Add the eggs, well beaten, and the flavouring.

Pour into a pie-dish, and bake for about thirty minutes.

Cold Tapioca Pudding.

Ingredients—5 tablespoonfuls of tapioca.

1 quart of milk.

4 tablespoonfuls of sugar.

Lemon, or some other flavouring.

Method.—Soak the tapioca all night in cold water.

The next day pour away the water, and put it, with the milk, into a large stewpan with the sugar.

Simmer gently for one hour.

Then pour it into a wetted basin, or mould.

When set, turn it out, and serve with stewed fruit, jam, or treacle.

Tapioca and Apples.

Ingredients—1 quart of water or milk.

4 tablespoonfuls of tapioca.

4 tablespoonfuls of sugar.

1 lb. of apples.

The grated rind of a lemon.

Method.—Soak the tapioca in cold water.

Then simmer it in the milk and water, with the sugar, for thirty minutes.

Add the apples, peeled, cored, and sliced.

Put the mixture into a pie-dish and bake for about one hour in a moderate oven.

Steamed Rice Pudding.

Ingredients—1 oz. of whole rice.

1 tablespoonful of sugar.

1 egg.

½ pint of milk.

Method.—Wash the rice well, and put it into a saucepan of cold water.

Bring it to the boil, and then pour off the water.

Pour in the milk, and add the sugar.

Simmer until the rice is quite soft.

Remove it from the fire, and when cooled a little, stir in the yolk of the egg.

Beat the white to a stiff froth, and stir it in lightly.

Put the mixture into a well-greased pudding-mould, and steam for thirty minutes.

Ratafia Pudding.

Ingredients—1 pint of milk.

3 eggs.

4 sponge cakes.

½ lb. of ratafias.

Method.—Boil the milk, and when it has cooled a little add to it the three eggs, well beaten.

Break the sponge cakes and ratafias in pieces, and pour the custard over them.

Decorate a greased mould with raisins, and pour the mixture into the mould.

Cover with greased paper, and steam for two hours.

Serve with sweet or wine sauce.

Macaroni Pudding.

Ingredients—½ lb. of macaroni.

¼ lb. of sugar.

1 or 2 eggs.

1 quart of milk.

Method.—Break the macaroni into pieces and put them into a saucepan of boiling water.

Boil for twenty minutes, and then strain off the water.

Pour in the milk; add the sugar, and simmer gently for ten minutes.

Beat up the eggs and stir them in.

Put the mixture into a buttered pie-dish and bake for about thirty minutes.

Eastern Pudding.

Ingredients—1 lb. of figs (cut in small dice).

¼ lb. of suet.

½ lb. of bread-crumbs.

2 eggs.

The grated rind of a lemon.

1 wineglass of brandy.

3 oz. of sugar.

Method.—Put the figs, suet, bread-crumbs, and grated lemon rind into a basin.

Mix it with the eggs, well beaten, and the brandy, adding a little milk if necessary.

Boil in a greased basin for two hours.

Ground-Barley Pudding.

Ingredients—1 tablespoonful of ground barley.

½ pint of milk.

1 tablespoonful of moist sugar.

1 egg.

Method.—Mix the barley smoothly with the milk.

Put it into a saucepan with the sugar, and bring to the boil, stirring all the time.

Then let it simmer for fifteen minutes.

Remove from the fire, and beat in the yolk of the egg.

Whip the white up stiffly, and stir in lightly.

Pour the mixture into a buttered pie-dish, and bake for fifteen minutes.

Steamed Semolina Pudding.

Ingredients—3 oz. of semolina.

1 pint of milk.

2 eggs.

2 oz. of moist sugar.

A little flavouring essence.

Method.—Boil the semolina in the milk, with the sugar, until quite soft.

Then add the flavouring essence and the yolks of the two eggs.

Beat the whites up stiffly and mix them in lightly.

Pour the mixture into a greased pudding-mould, and steam for one hour.

Albert Puddings.

Ingredients—4 oz. of flour.

4 oz. of butter.

4 oz. of castor sugar.

2 eggs.

A few drops of vanilla flavouring.

Method.—Work the butter to a cream in a basin, and beat in the flour, sugar, and eggs smoothly.

Add the flavouring essence.

Put the mixture into well-greased cups and bake for about half an hour.

Serve with sweet sauce.

Pearl-Barley Pudding.

Ingredients—1 oz. of pearl barley.

1 pint of milk.

2 oz. of moist sugar.

Method.—Put the barley to soak in cold water all night.

Then pour away the water and put the barley into a pie-dish.

Add the sugar and milk; and bake in a moderate oven for three hours.

Baked Lemon Pudding.

Ingredients—1 pint of milk.

3 oz. of bread-crumbs.

1 egg.

3 oz. of moist sugar.

The juice of a lemon and half the rind, grated.

Method.—Put the crumbs into a basin.

Boil the milk with the butter and sugar, and pour it over the crumbs.

Stir in the egg, well beaten; add the lemon rind and juice.

Pour it into a greased pie-dish, and bake in a moderate oven until set.

West-of-England Pudding.

Ingredients—3 tablespoonfuls of sago.

6 small apples.

1 quart of milk.

3 oz. of moist sugar.

Method.—Soak the sago in cold water for an hour.

Then simmer it in the milk, with the sugar, for twenty minutes.

Peel and core the apples.

Place them in a buttered pie-dish, and pour the sago over them.

Bake in a moderate oven for about one hour.

Pancakes.

Ingredients—½ lb. of flour.

2 eggs.

1 pint of milk.

Some lard, or dripping, for frying.

Method.—Put the flour into a basin, add to it a pinch of salt.

Make a well in the middle and put the two eggs into it; mix them smoothly with the flour; and add the milk very gradually.

Melt the lard, or dripping.

Well season a small frying-pan, about the size of a cheese plate.

Put into it a teaspoonful of the melted fat, and let it run well over the pan.

Then pour in enough batter to cover the pan thinly, and fry it brown, shaking the pan occasionally to keep it from burning.

Then toss it on to the other side; and, when that is fried, turn it on to kitchen paper.

Sprinkle with sugar and lemon juice and roll it up.

Keep it hot while the remainder of the batter is fried in the same way.

If the maker cannot toss the pancakes well, they may be turned with a broad-bladed knife. If they are fried in a larger pan, more fat must be used.

Railway Pudding.

Ingredients—¼ lb. of flour.

2 oz. of castor sugar.

2 eggs.

½ pint of milk.

2 teaspoonfuls of baking powder.

Method.—Mix the flour, sugar, and baking powder in a basin.

Beat the eggs well with the milk, and mix the pudding with them.

Pour into a well-greased Yorkshire-pudding tin; and bake for about thirty minutes.

When done, turn out and cut into squares.

Dish in a circle, with a little jam, or treacle, on each.

Poor Knight's Pudding.

Ingredients—Some small square slices of stale bread.

Castor sugar.

Method.—Fry the bread in hot fat (*see* French Frying).

Drain on kitchen paper.

Dish in the form of a wreath, the one leaning on the other, and put a little jam on each.

Gooseberry Fool.

Ingredients—1 quart of gooseberries.

¾ lb. of moist sugar.

½ pint of water.

1 pint of milk or cream.

Method.—Take the tops and stalks from the gooseberries, and boil them with the sugar and water until soft.

Rub them through a hair sieve.

Mix in the milk, or cream, gradually; and serve on a glass dish.

Apricot Pudding.

Ingredients—¼ lb. of finely-chopped suet.

½ lb. of bread-crumbs.

3 eggs.

8 tablespoonfuls of apricot jam.

1 glass of sherry.

2 oz. of sugar.

Method.—Put the suet, bread-crumbs, and sugar into a basin, and mix with the eggs, well beaten, apricot and sherry.

Put the mixture into a greased pudding-mould and boil for two hours.

Stale-Bread Pudding.

Ingredients—½ lb. scraps of bread.

1 quart of boiling milk.

2 eggs.

2 oz. of sugar.

¼ lb. of currants.

Method.—Soak the bread in cold water until soft.
Squeeze it quite dry, and beat up with a fork.
Pour the boiling milk over.
Stir in the sugar and eggs, well beaten.
Then stir in the currants.
Bake in a pie-dish for two hours.

Baked Plum Pudding.

Ingredients—¼ lb. of finely-chopped suet.
¾ lb. of flour.
¼ lb. of raisins, stoned and chopped.
¼ lb. of currants.
2 oz. of candied peel.
2 oz. of moist sugar.
1 egg.
2 teaspoonfuls of baking powder.
1 gill, or more, of milk.

Method.—Put all the dry ingredients into a basin, and mix with the egg and milk; it must be quite stiff.
Bake in a greased baking-tin for one hour.
For serving, cut into squares, and dust them over with castor sugar.

Treacle Pudding.

Ingredients—1 lb. of flour.
¼ lb of finely-chopped suet.

¼ lb. of treacle.

½ oz. of ground ginger.

1 egg.

2 oz. of moist sugar.

1½ gill of milk.

1 teaspoonful of baking powder.

Method.—Put the dry ingredients into a basin.

Mix with the treacle and the egg well beaten with the milk.

Boil in a greased basin for four hours.

The egg may be omitted, if liked.

Plum Pudding.

Ingredients—¼ lb. of finely-chopped suet.

¼ lb. of currants.

¼ lb. of raisins, stoned and chopped.

6 oz. of flour.

6 oz. of bread-crumbs.

2 oz. of candied peel.

3 oz. of sugar.

1 gill of milk.

2 eggs.

½ teaspoonful of baking powder.

Method.—Put the dry ingredients into a basin, and mix with the eggs and milk, well beaten together.

Boil in a cloth or basin for four hours.

Windsor Pudding.

Ingredients—2 oz. of semolina.
1 oz. of candied peel.
½ pint of milk.
¼ lb. of treacle.

Method.—Mix the milk smoothly with the semolina.
Then put it into a saucepan and stir until it thickens.
Add the treacle and candied peel; pour it into a pie-dish.
Bake for about thirty minutes.

Spring Pudding.

Ingredients—1 pint of gooseberries.
½ pint of milk.
4 oz. of moist sugar.
Slices of bread-and-butter.

Method.—Stew the gooseberries with a very little water and the sugar for ten minutes.
Dip the bread into the milk, and lay a slice at the bottom of a pie-dish.
Put a layer of gooseberries on it.
Then another slice of bread-and-butter and more gooseberries.
Continue in this manner until the dish is full.
Bake gently for one hour.

Gingerbread Pudding.

Ingredients—½ lb. of flour.

½ lb. of treacle.

¼ lb. of finely chopped suet.

3 teaspoonfuls of ground ginger.

½ teaspoonful of baking powder.

2 oz. of candied peel.

1 egg.

A little milk.

Method.—Put the dry ingredients into a basin.

Mix with the egg, well beaten, treacle and milk.

Boil in a greased basin for three hours.

Economical Bread Pudding.

Ingredients—½ lb. of scraps of bread.

¼ lb. of finely-chopped suet.

¼ lb. of currants.

3 oz. of moist sugar.

1 egg.

Method.—Soak the bread in cold water until soft; squeeze it quite dry.

Beat it up with a fork.

Add to it the suet, sugar, and currants, which should be well washed and dried.

Mix with the egg, well beaten.

Boil in a greased basin for an hour.

Economical Ginger Pudding.

Ingredients—½ lb. of scraps of bread.

¼ lb. of finely-chopped suet.

2 oz. of moist sugar.

2 tablespoonfuls of treacle.

3 teaspoonfuls of ground ginger.

Method.—Soak the bread in cold water until quite soft.

Squeeze it dry, and beat with a fork until quite fine.

Add the suet, sugar, and ginger, and mix with the treacle.

Boil in a greased basin for an hour.

Economical Fig Pudding.

Ingredients—½ lb. of scraps of bread.

¼ lb. of finely-chopped suet.

½ lb. of figs.

1 egg.

3 oz. of moist sugar.

Method.—Soak the bread in cold water until quite soft.

Squeeze it dry.

Add to it the suet, sugar, and figs, chopped small, and mix with beaten egg.

Boil in a greased basin for one hour.

Economical Lemon Pudding.

Make like preceding recipe, substituting the grated rind and juice of two lemons for the figs.

Currant Pudding.

Ingredients—3 eggs.

The same weight of sugar, flour, and bread-crumbs.

Suet, currants, minced apples.

A little grated lemon rind.

A little milk.

Method.—Chop the suet finely, and add to it the sugar, flour, bread-crumbs, minced apple, currants, and grated lemon rind.

Mix with the eggs, well beaten, and a little milk.

Boil in a greased basin for three hours.

Plain Cold Cabinet Pudding.

Ingredients—1 tablespoonful of flour.

1½ tablespoonful of arrowroot.

1 wineglass of sherry.

A few raisins.

3 stale sponge cakes.

1 pint of milk.

2 oz. of sugar.

Method.—Put the milk to boil with the sugar.

When boiling, stir in the flour, mixed with a little cold milk.

When it thickens, add the arrowroot, also mixed smoothly with milk.

Boil for three minutes, stirring all the time.

Then add to it the sherry.

Cut the raisins in two and stone them.

Decorate a plain round tin with them.

Break up the cakes and put some pieces in the tin.

Pour in some of the thickened milk, then some more pieces of cake, and more milk.

Continue in this way until the mould is full.

Set it aside until quite cold.

Then turn it out, and serve with jam.

Cornflour Pudding.

Ingredients—2 tablespoonfuls of cornflour.

1 pint of milk.

2 tablespoonfuls of castor sugar.

1 egg, if liked.

Method.—Put the milk on to boil.

Put the cornflour into a pie-dish with the sugar.

Mix smoothly with a little cold milk.

Pour on it the boiling milk, stirring quickly until it thickens.

Add the egg, well beaten, and a little flavouring essence.

Bake in a pie-dish for about thirty minutes.

Swiss Pudding.

Ingredients—2 lb. of apples.

½ lb. of bread-crumbs.

3 oz. of moist sugar.

A little grated lemon rind.

1 oz. of butter.

Method.—Peel, core, and slice the apples.

Put a layer of them into a buttered pie-dish.

Sprinkle them with crumbs, lemon rind, and a little sugar, and put small pieces of butter about them.

Put some pieces of apple on the top; sprinkle them also with crumbs, lemon rind, sugar, and butter.

Continue in the same way until the dish is full.

Bake until the pudding is nicely browned.

For serving, it may be turned out of the dish.

Brown-Bread Pudding.

Ingredients—1 loaf of brown bread.

1 gill of double cream.

The rind of 1 lemon.

3 oz. of castor sugar.

1 gill of milk.

4 eggs.

A few drops of essence of vanilla.

Method.—Remove the crust from the loaf, and rub the crumb through a wire sieve.

Put five ounces of the crumbs into a basin with the sugar and grated lemon rind.

Boil the milk, pour it over the crumbs, and add the vanilla essence.

Whip the cream to a stiff froth, and mix it with the pudding, adding also the yolks of the eggs.

Beat the whites of two eggs to a stiff froth, and stir them in lightly.

Put the mixture into a well-greased mould, and steam for an hour and a half.

Diplomatic Pudding.

Ingredients—¼ pint of sweet jelly.

1 pint of milk.

½ oz. of gelatine.

2 sponge cakes.

2 oz. of ratafias.

1 whole egg, and 4 yolks.

2 oz. of sugar.

A little flavouring essence.

Method.—Soak the gelatine in a little milk.

Break the sponge cakes and ratafias, and put them into a basin.

Boil the milk with the sugar.

Beat the eggs, and pour the milk on them.

Strain it into a jug, and put it to stand in a saucepan of boiling water, and stir until the custard coats the spoon.

Then melt the gelatine, add it to the custard, and pour it at once over the cakes.

While the mixture cools, pour a little jelly, coloured with cochineal, into a plain round tin.

When it is set, place a jam-pot, or a smaller tin, on it, and pour some jelly round the sides.

When it is quite firm, pour some boiling water into the jam-pot, or tin, and remove it quickly.

When the custard and cakes are cold, but not set, add the essence, and pour into the mould.

When quite firm, dip the tin in hot water for a second or two, and turn it on to a glass dish.

Pease Pudding.

Ingredients—1 pint of split peas.

Pepper and salt.

Method.—Soak the peas overnight.

Tie them in a bag or cloth, leaving room for them to swell.

Cook them with the meat with which they are to be served.

Then drain them in a colander.

Mash them with pepper and salt, and press them into a shape in a vegetable-dish.

Hominy Porridge.

Ingredients—1 pint of milk or water.

3 tablespoonfuls of flaked hominy.

Method.—Mix the hominy smoothly with the milk or water.

Stir and cook over the fire for ten minutes.

Hominy Pudding.

Ingredients—3 tablespoonfuls of flaked hominy.

1 pint of milk.

2 tablespoonfuls of sugar.

Method.—Mix the hominy with a little cold milk, and make the remainder boil.

Then stir in the hominy and cook until it thickens.

Add the sugar, pour into a greased pie-dish, and bake for about half an hour.

If liked, one or two eggs may be added to the pudding, with a little flavouring essence.

NOTE.—The *flaked* hominy is the best for general purposes, as the *granulated* takes many hours boiling before it is properly cooked.

VEGETABLES.

The rules for cooking vegetables are very simple, and easily remembered. All vegetables, with the exception of old potatoes, are put into boiling water. Green vegetables must be boiled with the lid off the saucepan, as the steam would discolour them, and the water must *boil, not simmer*. Salt is added, in the proportion of one tablespoonful to every two quarts of water. If the water is very hard, it may be necessary to add a little piece of soda. The lime in hard water discolours green vegetables, and the use of soda is to throw this down. Do not, however, use soda, unless obliged, as too much of it will destroy, to some extent, the flavour of the vegetables. Peas must be boiled gently, as rapid boiling would break their skins. Haricot beans must be boiled gently, for the same reason. Root vegetables take longer to cook than fresh ones. Old potatoes must be put into warm water, as they require gradual cooking, and must be boiled gently, until tender. With that exception, all the others must be put into boiling water. Carrots, turnips, and parsnips are generally cooked with the meat with which they are served, as their flavour is thereby improved.

To Boil Potatoes.

If boiled in their skins, scrub them perfectly clean, and put them into a saucepan with sufficient warm water to cover them.

Sprinkle them with salt and boil them gently for half an hour or more, until very *nearly* tender, but not quite.

Then pour the water away.

Peel the potatoes, replace them in the saucepan, sprinkle salt upon them, cover them with a cloth, and put the lid on the saucepan.

Let them stand by the side of the fire to finish cooking in their own steam.

Care must be taken that the potatoes cooked in this way are free from disease. One tainted potato would destroy the flavour of the others.

If cooked without their skins, pare them thinly and treat them in the same manner, pouring off the water when they are very nearly tender, and finish cooking them in their own steam.

If the potatoes are good and are cooked according to these directions, they will be perfectly dry and flowery.

To Steam Potatoes.

Put the potatoes into the steamer, and sprinkle them with salt.

Keep the water in the saucepan underneath quickly boiling the whole time the potatoes are cooking.

If the potatoes are cooked in their skins,[*] peel them when very nearly tender, and put them back in the steamer to finish cooking.

Steaming is one of the simplest and best ways of cooking potatoes. If the potatoes are good and the water is kept briskly boiling, this method cannot fail to be successful.

To Cook New Potatoes.

Put the potatoes into boiling water with some salt, and boil gently for twenty minutes or more, according to their age.

When very nearly tender pour off the water, cover them with a cloth, and set the saucepan by the side of the fire, and finish cooking in their own steam.

Baked Potatoes.

Choose nice potatoes, not too large, and scrub them perfectly clean.

Bake them in a moderate oven for about an hour.

Brussels Sprouts.

Trim them nicely and put them in boiling water, adding salt in the proportion of a tablespoonful to every two quarts of water.

Put in a little sugar, or, if the water is hard, a little piece of soda the size of a pea.

Boil them quickly, with the lid off the saucepan, from ten to twenty minutes, according to the size and age of the sprouts.

When tender, drain them quite dry in a colander.

Dry the saucepan and put them back with a little butter, pepper, and salt.

Shake them over the fire for a minute or so, and then serve on a hot dish.

To Boil a Cauliflower.

Soak it in salt and water to draw out any insects, and trim off the outside leaves.

Put it, with the flower downwards, into a saucepan of boiling water with salt in it, and cook from twenty to thirty minutes, according to its age.

Drain it on a sieve or colander.

If liked, it may be served with white or French sauce poured over it (*see* Sauces.)

Green Peas.

Put them into plenty of boiling water, with a little sugar and a sprig or two of mint.

Boil gently with the lid off the saucepan for twenty minutes or more, according to their size and age.

Drain them in a colander.

Then put them into a saucepan with a little piece of butter, a teaspoonful of castor sugar, pepper and salt, and shake them over the fire for a minute or two.

French Beans.

Remove the strings and cut the beans into slices.

Put them into plenty of boiling water, with salt in the proportion of one tablespoonful to every two quarts of water, a little sugar, or, if the water is hard, a small piece of soda about the size of a pea.

Boil quickly for fifteen minutes or longer, according to their age.

Drain in a colander.

Then put them into a saucepan with a small piece of butter, pepper and salt, and shake them over the fire for a minute or two.

Spinach.

Pull off the stalks and wash the spinach well in several waters to remove all grit.

Put it into a saucepan without any water but that which adheres to the leaves, and sprinkle a little salt over it.

Cook with the lid off the saucepan until quite tender, stirring it occasionally.

Drain it in a colander, and wring it dry in a cloth.

Then chop it, or rub it through a wire sieve. The latter method is preferable.

To dress it, mix it in a saucepan over the fire with a little butter, pepper, and salt; a little cream may be used also, care being taken not to make the spinach too moist to serve.

Press it into shape, as a mound or pyramid, in a vegetable dish, and garnish with fried *croutons* of bread.

Asparagus.

Cut the asparagus all the same length, and scrape the white part lightly.

Tie it together and put it in boiling water, to which salt has been added, in the proportion of one tablespoonful to two quarts of water.

Add also half an ounce of butter.

Boil gently with the lid off the saucepan for half an hour, until the green part is tender—very young asparagus will not take so long.

Dish on toast; if liked, French or white sauce may be poured over the green ends.

Jerusalem Artichokes.

Peel them, and throw them into boiling water, with salt in the proportion of one tablespoonful to every two quarts of water.

Boil gently with the lid on the saucepan for about fifteen or twenty minutes, until quite tender.

They may be served plain, or with French or white sauce poured over them.

They should be sent to table quickly, or they will be discoloured.

Carrots.

Scrape them and put them into boiling water with salt in it, in the proportion of one tablespoonful to every two quarts of water.

Boil gently with the lid on the saucepan until they are quite tender.

New carrots will take about twenty minutes, old ones an hour or more, according to their age and size.

When they are served with boiled meat, they are generally cooked with it. New carrots are sometimes boiled in second stock.

When tender, they are put on a hot vegetable dish, the stock is rapidly boiled down to a glaze, and poured over them.

Turnips.

Boil according to directions given for cooking carrots. Turnips generally take about half an hour; but the time depends on their age and size. If liked, they may be rubbed through a wire sieve, and mashed with butter, pepper, and salt.

Parsnips.

Cook like carrots. They may be served plain, or rubbed through a wire sieve and mashed with butter, pepper, and salt.

Haricot Beans.

Soak them overnight.

Put them into boiling water with a small piece of butter and a small onion.

Boil gently from three to four hours until quite tender.

Drain them, and before serving shake them over the fire with a little butter, pepper, and salt.

Spanish Onions.

First blanch them by putting them into cold water and bringing it to the boil.

Then throw away the water.

Rinse the onions, sprinkle some salt over them, and put them into fresh water.

Boil gently from two to three hours, until perfectly tender.

Drain them, and serve, if liked, with French, Italian or white sauce.

Spanish onions are sometimes boiled in stock, or milk which is afterwards used to make the sauce.

Celery.

Clean the celery thoroughly, and tie it in bundles.

Put it in boiling water, milk, or stock, with a little salt and butter, and simmer gently for twenty minutes or more, until quite tender.

Dish on a piece of toast.

If liked, a sauce may be made with the liquor in which the celery has been cooked, and poured over it.

Vegetable Marrows.

Peel the marrows thinly, and cut them in quarters, removing the seeds.

Put them in boiling water, with salt in the proportion of one tablespoonful to every two quarts of water, and boil gently until tender.

They may be served, if desired, with French or white sauce poured over them.

Marrows are very nice when boiled in milk; the milk can afterwards be used to make the sauce.

Cabbage.

Take off the outer decayed leaves, and soak the cabbage in salt and water, to draw out any insects. If very large, cut into quarters.

Put into boiling water, to which salt should be added, in the proportion of a tablespoonful to every two quarts of water. If the water is hard, a piece of soda the size of a bean should be added.

Boil quickly—with the lid off the saucepan—for half an hour, or more, until tender.

Drain well in a colander before serving.

Broad Beans.

Put them, when shelled, into boiling water, to which salt should be added in the proportion of a tablespoonful to every two quarts of water.

Boil gently, from fifteen minutes to half an hour, according to their size and age.

When tender, pour the water away, and shake them in the saucepan over the fire, with a little butter or dripping, pepper, and salt.

Tomatoes.

These are better baked than boiled: boiling destroys their flavour.

Put them on a baking-tin, greased with butter or dripping.

Sprinkle over them a little pepper and salt, and cover them with a greased paper.

Put them in a moderate oven, for about ten minutes or a quarter of an hour.

Seakale.

Tie it in bundles, and put into boiling water, with a little butter, and also some salt, in the proportion of a tablespoonful to every two quarts of water.

Boil, with the lid off the saucepan, until the seakale is tender.

Drain, and serve on toast. French or white sauce may be poured over it.

Seakale is sometimes boiled in milk, which should afterwards be used to make the sauce.

Mushrooms.

Peel the mushrooms; rinse them to remove any grit, and cut off the ends of the stalks.

Put them on a greased baking-tin, with the stalks upwards, and put some little bits of butter on each mushroom, with a little pepper and salt.

Cover them with buttered paper, and bake them in a moderate oven from ten to twenty minutes, until tender.

Serve on a hot dish, with the gravy poured over them.

Stewed Mushrooms.

Peel and rinse the mushrooms, and cut off the ends of the stalks.

Stew them gently in water, stock, or milk, until quite tender, adding pepper and salt to taste.

Then thicken the gravy with a little flour, and let it cook well, stirring carefully.

Before serving, stir in a little cream or butter.

Fried Potatoes.

Take thin peelings of potatoes, and twist into fancy shapes, or cut the potatoes into thin slices.

Dry them well in a cloth, and drop them into hot fat (*see* French Frying) until quite crisp, and of a light brown colour.

Remove them with a fish-slice or colander-spoon, and drain them on kitchen paper.

Tomato Farni.

Ingredients—6 or 8 ripe tomatoes.

1 oz. of butter.

½ oz. of flour.

1 gill of stock or milk.

1 dessertspoonful of chopped parsley.

1 dessertspoonful of chopped cooked ham.

1 dessertspoonful of grated Parmesan cheese.

A few button mushrooms, chopped.

A few drops of lemon juice.

Some white and browned bread-crumbs.

Pepper and salt.

Method.—Melt the butter in a small stewpan.

Mix in the flour smoothly.

Then add the stock or milk; stir and cook well.

Then mix in sufficient white bread-crumbs to make the mixture stiff.

Add the parsley, mushrooms, cheese, ham, lemon-juice, pepper, and salt.

Scoop out the top of each tomato.

Pile a little of the stuffing on each, and sprinkle a few browned bread-crumbs over.

Put them on a greased baking-sheet, and cook them in a moderate oven for about a quarter of an hour.

Cauliflower au gratin.

Ingredients—1 cauliflower.

1 oz. of butter.

1 oz. of flour.

1 gill of water.

2 tablespoonfuls of cream.

2 oz. of grated Parmesan cheese.

Pepper, salt, and a little cayenne.

Method.—Boil the cauliflower; remove the green leaves.

Place it, with the flower upwards, in a vegetable-dish, and press it into an oval shape.

Melt the butter in a small stewpan.

Mix the flour in smoothly.

Add the water; stir and cook well.

Then add the cream, and one ounce of Parmesan cheese, pepper, salt, and cayenne.

Pour the sauce over the cauliflower.

Sprinkle the remainder of the cheese over it, and brown, either with a salamander or in a quick oven.

Potato Croquettes.

Ingredients—2 lb. of potatoes.

2 oz. of butter.

2 eggs.

Pepper and salt.

Some white bread-crumbs.

Method.—Boil the potatoes, and rub them through a wire sieve.

Mash them well with the butter, pepper, and salt.

Mix in one egg, well beaten.

Flour the hands very slightly, and form the mixture in balls, or any other shape preferred.

Brush them over with beaten egg, and cover them with crumbs.

Slightly mould them again when the crumbs are on them.

Fry in a frying-basket, in hot fat (*see* French Frying).

Garnish with fried parsley.

Salsify Patties.

Ingredients—Some patty-cases, made as for oysters.

½ lb. of salsify.

1 oz. of flour.

½ pint of milk.

2 tablespoonfuls of cream.

A few drops of lemon juice.

Pepper and salt.

A little cayenne.

Method.—Cook the salsify in milk or water until tender.

Then cut it into small pieces.

Melt the butter in a small stewpan, mix in the flour smoothly.

Then add the milk; stir and cook well.

Mix in the cream and let it boil in the sauce.

Then add the lemon juice, seasoning, and salsify.

Fill the patty-cases with the mixture, and put a lid on each.

Tomatoes au gratin.

Ingredients—1½ lb. of tomatoes.

1 pint of bread-crumbs.

2 oz. of butter.

Pepper and salt to taste.

Method.—Slice the tomatoes, and put a layer of them in the bottom of a pie-dish.

Cover them with crumbs; sprinkle with pepper and salt, and place small pieces of butter on them.

Then put another layer of tomatoes, covering them in the same way with crumbs.

Use up all the tomatoes and crumbs in this way, letting the last layer be of crumbs.

Bake in a quick oven for about twenty minutes.

Mashed Potatoes.

Ingredients—1 oz. of butter to every pound of potatoes.

1 tablespoonful of cream, if possible.

Pepper and salt to taste.

Method.—The potatoes should be well cooked, and be dry and floury.

Put them quickly through a wire sieve.

Mix them well in a saucepan with the butter, cream, and seasoning.

Make them quite hot.

Heap them in a mound-like form in a vegetable dish, and smooth over with a knife.

Mashed Potatoes (a plainer way).

Add to the potatoes, while in the saucepan, some butter or dripping.

Season with pepper and salt.

Beat with a fork until perfectly smooth and free from lumps.

Where economy must be studied, nice beef dripping will be found an excellent substitute for butter.

Potato Balls.

Form some mashed potatoes into balls.

Brush them over with beaten egg.

Put them on a greased baking-tin, and bake in a quick oven until brown.

Serve garnished with parsley.

This is a nice way of using up cold potatoes.

Flaked Potatoes.

Rub some nicely-cooked floury potatoes through a wire sieve into a hot vegetable dish. This must be done quickly, that the potatoes may be served quite hot.

Rice for a Curry.

Well wash some Patna rice. Throw it into plenty of quickly-boiling water with salt in it, and boil until the rice is nearly cooked, but not quite. This will take from eight to ten minutes. Strain the rice on a sieve and pour hot water over it, rinsing it well. Then put it in the saucepan again, cover it and let it stand in a hot place to finish cooking in its own steam.

SOUPS.

These are very valuable preparations, and are useful to the poor as well as to the rich, as many of the most nutritious soups are the cheapest. Pea soup, haricot soup, and lentil soup are all rich in nourishment, and may be made at a trifling cost, stock not being *necessary* for their manufacture. The boilings from meat, when not too salt, may be used with advantage in making these soups; but if this is not available, they may be made quite well with water; and, if carefully prepared, will have all the flavour of a meat soup.

In making stock for meat soups, it must be borne in mind that in order to extract the juices from the meat it must be put into *cold* water, which should be heated very gradually, and only allowed to *simmer*. In this way a rich stock is procured, as all the virtue of the meat is drawn into the water. Boiling would produce a poor and flavourless stock, as the extreme heat applied, by hardening the albumen, would tend to keep in the juices of the meat instead of drawing them out.

In making stock from bones, the method to be pursued is quite the opposite. Bones must be boiled, otherwise the gelatine in them will not be extracted; simmering would be of little use. The gelatine can only be thoroughly extracted when they are boiled at higher pressure than is possible in ordinary cookery. Bones contain so much gelatine that after they have been once used in stock they should be broken up in pieces and again boiled, so that the gelatine from the *inside* may also be extracted.

An economical cook will often make excellent stock for soup from bones alone, with the addition of suitable vegetables for flavouring.

First Stock for Clear Soup.

Ingredients—4 lb. of shin of beef, or 2 lb. of shin of beef and 2 lb. of knuckle of veal.

5 pints of water.

2 carrots.

2 turnips.

1 onion.

The white part of a leek.

1 dozen peppercorns.

1 sprig of parsley, thyme, and marjoram.

A bay leaf.

Pepper and salt.

Method.—Cut the meat into pieces about one inch in size.

Break up the bone and remove the marrow.

Put bones and meat into a stockpot with the cold water.

Let them soak for half an hour.

Then put the pot on the fire; add some salt and pepper to it, and gently simmer the contents for half an hour.

Next put in the vegetables sliced, and the herbs tied together.

Simmer for 4½ hours longer, skimming occasionally.

Strain into a clean pan, and set aside to get cold.

White Stock.

This may be made by the directions in the preceding recipe, using white meat instead of beef; knuckle of veal is considered the stock meat for white soup. Knuckle of veal and a rabbit make excellent stock.

Very good economical white stock may be made by using bones only in making the stock, and no meat; use a ham-bone, if possible, with the others, as this gives a nice flavour.

Second Stock.

Take any scraps of cooked or uncooked meat; any bones, cooked or uncooked, to make second stock. Allow one pint of water to every pound of meat and bones, and vegetables in the same proportion as for first stock. The bones should be broken up. Boil gently until all the virtue is extracted from the meat, bones, and vegetables. The contents of the stockpot should be emptied into a pan every night, and the stock strained from the meat, bones, and vegetables. These should be looked over, and the bones, meat, &c., which are of no further use removed; the remainder should be set aside to use with fresh stock material. Bones may be boiled for a very long time before the gelatine will be perfectly extracted.

Second stock, when cold, should be a stiff jelly, in consequence of the gelatine contained in the bones.

White Stock from Bones uncooked.

Ingredients—4 lb. of uncooked bones, with a ham-bone, if possible, amongst them.

5 pints of water.

2 carrots.

2 turnips.

1 large onion.

Half a head of celery.

1 sprig of parsley.

Thyme, marjoram, and a bay leaf.

1 blade of mace.

Method.—Break up the bones and put them with the vegetables, sliced, into a stockpot with the water; boil gently for five hours, adding pepper and salt to taste. Then strain into a clean pan.

Clear Soup.

Ingredients—2 quarts of first stock.

¾ lb. of gravy beef.

The white and shell of one egg.

Method.—Remove *all* the fat from the stock. If it is in a jelly, take off as much as possible with an iron spoon, and remove the remainder by washing the top of the stock with a cloth dipped in very hot water.

Scrape the beef finely and soak it in two tablespoonfuls of cold water to loosen the juices.

Put the stock in a stewpan and add the beef to it, the white and shell of the egg, and a very tiny piece of each kind of vegetable used in making the stock.

Whisk over the fire until the stock begins to simmer.

Then leave off stirring and let it well boil up.

Remove it from the fire and put it on one side for a crust to form.

Tie a clean cloth to the four legs of a chair turned upside down.

Pour some boiling water through it into a basin, to ensure it being perfectly clean.

Then put a clean basin underneath and pour all the contents of the stewpan on to the cloth. The first time the soup runs through it will be cloudy, because the filter made by the beef and egg will not have settled at the bottom of the cloth.

Take the soup away; put a clean basin under the cloth, and pour the soup slowly through.

If this is carefully done the soup will be quite brilliant the second time of straining, and will not require to go through the cloth again.

Julienne Soup.

This is a clear soup with shred vegetables served in it.

Scrape some carrots and take thin parings of them.

Cut these into very thin strips.

Take some thin slices of turnip and cut them into strips of the same length.

Boil the turnips for five minutes, and the carrots for fifteen minutes.

Consommée au Royal.

This is clear soup with a savoury custard in it.

Savoury Custard.

Ingredients—1 whole egg.

1 yolk.

½ gill of clear soup.

Pepper and salt to taste.

Method.—Beat the eggs and soup together and strain them into a greased gallipot.

Cover them with buttered paper and steam very gently for a quarter of an hour until the custard is firm.

Let it cool, then turn it out. Cut into thin slices.

Stamp into dice or diamonds and serve them in the clear soup.

If the custard is not very gently steamed it will be full of holes, and useless for this purpose.

Consommée à la Princesse.

Serve small *quenelles* (see Quenelles of Veal), made in teaspoons, and nicely poached, in the clear soup.

Friar Tuck.

Make one quart of clear soup boiling hot. Beat two eggs well. When the soup is quite boiling, strain the eggs through a pointed strainer into it.

Celery Soup.

Ingredients—2 quarts of second stock.

4 heads of celery.

4 oz. of flour.

½ pint of cream or good milk.

Method.—Wash the celery well and cut it in pieces.

Simmer it in the stock for half an hour or more until quite tender.

Make a thickening of the flour; pour it into the soup and boil, stirring, for three minutes.

Then rub through a sieve.

Put it into the saucepan again.

Add the cream, stir and let it boil up.

Serve with fried *croutons* of bread.

Oyster Soup.

Ingredients—2 dozen oysters.

1½ pint of white stock.

2 oz. of butter.

2 oz. of flour.

1 teaspoonful of anchovy sauce.

A few drops of lemon juice.

Pepper and salt.

Method.—Beard the oysters and cut them in two.

Put the beards into the stock and simmer them in it for a few minutes.

Melt the butter in another stewpan; mix in the flour smoothly; pour in the stock; stir and boil well.

Add the cream and let it boil in the soup.

Strain the oyster liquor and scald the oysters in it.

Put them in the soup and add the anchovy sauce and lemon juice.

Haricot Soup.

Ingredients—1 pint of haricot beans.

1 onion.

2 quarts of water.

1 pint of milk.

½ oz. of dripping.

Pepper and salt to taste.

Method.—Soak the beans over night in cold water.

Boil them with the onion, dripping, pepper and salt, in three pints of water, from three to four hours, until quite soft.

Rub them with their liquor through a wire sieve.

Add the milk, and make the soup hot, stirring it over the fire until it boils.

Serve with fried *croutons* of bread.

Note.—This soup is much improved if it is rubbed through a *hair* sieve after it has been through the wire sieve.

Green Pea Purée.

Ingredients—2 pints of shelled peas.

A large handful of pea-shells.

2 or 3 leaves of spinach.

2 or 3 sprigs of parsley.

A few young onions.

A sprig of mint.

A small piece of soda.

1 lump of sugar.

3 pints of second stock.

2 tablespoonfuls of arrowroot.

Pepper and salt to taste.

Method.—Wash the shells well, and put them, with the peas and other vegetables, into boiling water, to which is added the soda and the sugar.

When quite tender, drain off the water, and put the vegetables into the stock, which should be made boiling.

Let it boil up.

Then rub through a hair sieve.

Make the soup hot; thicken with arrow-root; and, in serving, add, if liked, a little cream, or glaze.

Potage à l'Américaine.

Ingredients—3 pints of second stock.

2 tablespoonfuls of crushed tapioca.

8 good-sized tomatoes.

Method.—Put the stock into a stewpan on the fire to boil.

When boiling, stir in the crushed tapioca.

Stir and cook for about ten minutes, until it is transparent.

Rub the tomatoes through a hair sieve.

Add them to the stock.

Boil for about two minutes and the soup will be ready to serve.

Cream may be added if liked.

Onion Soup.

Ingredients—6 Spanish onions.

3 oz. of butter.

2 quarts of water.

3 oz. of flour.

½ pint of milk or cream.

Pepper and salt to taste.

Method.—Peel the onions, and cut them in slices.

Fry them in the butter, but do not let them discolour.

Then boil them in the water until quite soft.

Rub them with their liquor through a hair sieve.

Put this *purée* into a stewpan on the fire to boil.

When boiling, stir in a thickening of the flour.

Stir and cook well.

Then add the milk or cream, pepper, and salt, to taste.

Let the soup boil up, and it is ready.

Serve with fried *croutons* of bread.

Tapioca Cream.

Ingredients—1½ pint of white stock.

1 oz. of crushed tapioca.

2 tablespoonfuls of cream.

The yolks of 2 eggs.

Pepper and salt to taste.

Method.—Put the stock into a stewpan on the fire to boil.

When boiling, sprinkle in the crushed tapioca.

Stir and cook well for about ten minutes.

Beat the yolks lightly with the cream, and strain them.

Let the stock cool a little, and then add two or three tablespoonfuls of it gradually to the eggs and cream.

Pour the eggs and cream into the stock, and stir over the fire until the eggs thicken like custard.

Care must be taken that the stock does not boil after the eggs are in it, as that would curdle them.

Palestine Soup.

Ingredients—3 lb. of Jerusalem artichokes.
2 quarts of stock; or the liquor mutton or veal has been boiled in.
1 onion.
1 turnip.
½ head of celery.
½ pint of cream, or good milk.
Pepper and salt to taste.

Method.—Peel and cut the artichokes and other vegetables into slices.
Boil them in the stock until tender.
Rub through a hair sieve.
Add the cream, and boil it in the soup.
Add pepper and salt; and serve with fried *croutons* of bread.

Potato Purée.

Ingredients—1 lb. of potatoes.
1 onion.
1 stick of celery.
1½ pint of white stock.
½ pint of cream or milk.
Pepper and salt to taste.

Method.—Peel the potatoes, and cut them, as well as the onion and the celery, into thin slices.
Put them in the stock, and simmer gently until tender.
Rub through a tammy-cloth or hair sieve.
Add the cream to the soup, and make it hot.

Serve with fried *croutons* of bread.

Egyptian Purée or Lentil Soup.

Ingredients—1 pint of Egyptian lentils.

1 good-sized onion.

Carrot and turnip.

3 sticks of celery, or one dessertspoonful of celery seed tied in a piece of muslin.

2 quarts of water, or liquor from a leg of mutton.

Pepper and salt.

Method.—Wash the lentils thoroughly.

Then boil them in the water with the vegetables, cut in small pieces, from two to three hours, stirring occasionally; when quite cooked, rub through a wire sieve; season to taste.

Make the soup hot in a stewpan, stirring all the time.

Serve with fried *croutons* of bread.

NOTE.—This soup is much improved if it is rubbed through a hair sieve, after it has been through the wire sieve.

Pea Soup.

Make according to directions given in preceding recipe, substituting split peas for lentils.

Calf-tail Soup.

Ingredients—4 calves' tails.

1 carrot.

1 turnip.

1 onion.

1 sprig of thyme, parsley, and marjoram.

A little celery.

1 small clove of garlic.

1 dozen peppercorns.

4 oz. flour.

2 quarts of stock.

Salt.

Method.—Cut the tails into joints.

Put them into a stewpan, with the water; when it simmers put in the vegetables, &c., and cook very gently for four hours.

Remove the pieces of tail, and let the stock get cold.

Then remove the fat, and thicken the stock with the flour.

Serve with the pieces of tail in it. A wineglass of sherry may be added if liked.

Ox-tail Soup.

Ingredients—1 ox-tail.

3 quarts of stock.

1 carrot, 1 turnip, and 1 onion.

Half a head of celery.

1 slice of ham.

1 sprig of parsley, thyme, and marjoram.

2 bay leaves.

3 cloves.

Pepper and salt.

2 oz. of butter.

1 wineglass of sherry.

A few drops of lemon juice.

4 oz. of flour.

Method.—Cut the ox-tail into joints.

Fry them in the butter, with the vegetables, cut in pieces.

Put the tail and vegetables into a large saucepan with the stock, pepper, salt, and cloves.

Boil for very nearly four hours.

Then strain the stock.

Remove the pieces of tail, and put them on one side.

When the stock is quite cold, remove the fat perfectly and put the stock in a stewpan on the fire to boil.

When it boils, stir in a thickening made of the flour.

Stir, and cook the flour well.

Then add the sherry and lemon juice. Serve with the pieces of tail in it.

Sheep's-head Soup.

Ingredients—1 sheep's head.

3 quarts of water.

1 large carrot.

1 large turnip.

1 large onion.

1 sprig of parsley, thyme, and marjoram.

1 head of celery.

4 oz. of flour.

1 teaspoonful of minced parsley.

2 tablespoonfuls of bread-crumbs.

1 egg.

Pepper and salt.

Method.—Split open the head, and clean it thoroughly.

Remove the tongue and brains, and blanch the head by putting it into cold water and bringing it to the boil.

Throw the water away, and rinse the head well.

Put it into a large saucepan with the three quarts of water and the vegetables, cut in small pieces.

Boil gently for five hours.

Then strain into a basin, and rub the meat and vegetables through a wire sieve.

When cold, remove the fat from the stock, and add the pulped vegetables and meat.

Make the soup hot, and stir in a thickening made of the flour.

Boil the flour well, stirring all the time.

Serve the soup with forcemeat balls in it.

To make the Forcemeat Balls.—Boil the tongue and brains separately.

Chop them up; mix them with the bread-crumbs, pepper, salt, and the minced parsley, and bind with the egg.

Make into balls, and roll them in flour; place them on a greased baking-sheet and bake until brown.

Put them in a soup-tureen, and pour the soup over them.

Tapioca Soup.

Ingredients—2 oz. of tapioca.

4 pints of second stock.

Method.—Wash the tapioca well, and throw it into the stock when boiling.

Simmer gently for half an hour, stirring occasionally.

Ox-cheek Soup.

Ingredients—1 ox-cheek.

Some cold water, allowing 1 pint to every pound of meat and 1 quart over.

2 carrots.

2 turnips.

2 onions.

Half a head of celery.

1 sprig of parsley, thyme, and marjoram.

2 bay leaves.

Pepper and salt.

Flour.

If possible, a ham-bone.

A few drops of lemon juice.

Method.—Cut up the cheek, and put it with the bone and vegetables into a stockpot to boil gently for five hours, skimming occasionally.

Then strain the stock into a clean pan and set it aside to get cold.

When cold, carefully remove all the fat.

Put the stock into a stewpan on the fire to boil.

When boiling, stir in a thickening made of the flour, mixed smoothly with cold water. Use one ounce of flour to every pint of stock.

Stir and boil the flour in the stock for three minutes.

Add to it a squeeze of lemon juice, and serve the soup with neat pieces of the cheek, about one inch in size, in it.

The remains of the cheek may be reboiled, with fresh vegetables, to make a plain second stock.

Giblet Soup.

Ingredients—2 sets of goose or 4 sets of duck giblets.

¼ of a head of celery.

1 carrot.

1 turnip.

1 onion.

2 cloves.

1 blade of mace.

1 sprig of parsley, thyme, and marjoram.

2 quarts of second stock.

A few drops of lemon juice.

Pepper and salt.

Method.—Clean the giblets thoroughly, and cut them in pieces.

Put them into a saucepan, with the vegetables sliced, and the stock, and simmer gently for two hours.

Then take out the best pieces of giblet, trim them neatly, and set them aside.

Simmer the soup for half an hour longer.

Then add to it a thickening of flour, using one ounce of flour to every pint of stock.

Boil and cook the flour well, and add pepper and salt to taste.

Strain the soup into another saucepan.

Add to it the lemon juice, and, if liked, two glasses of Madeira wine; also the pieces of giblet.

Make it quite hot, and it is then ready for serving.

Milk Soup.

Ingredients—4 potatoes.

2 onions.

2 oz. of butter or dripping.

3 tablespoonfuls of semolina.

1 pint of milk.

2 quarts of liquor from meat.

Pepper and salt to taste.

Method.—Slice the potatoes and onions; add them to the meat liquor, with the butter and pepper and salt to taste, and boil gently for one hour.

Then rub the soup through a wire sieve.

Put it into the saucepan again, and, when boiling, shake into it the semolina and cook for fifteen minutes, stirring occasionally.

When the semolina is cooked the soup is ready.

If this soup is used for children, water may be substituted for the meat liquor if the latter is not available.

Bonne Femme Soup.

Ingredients—2 lettuces.

2 leaves of sorrel.

4 sprigs of taragon.

2 sprigs of chervil.

Half a cucumber.

2 pints of white stock.

The yolks of 3 eggs.

¼ of a pint of cream.

The crust of a French roll.

½ oz. of butter.

Method.—Wash the lettuce, taragons, and chervil well, and shred them finely.

Peel the cucumber, and shred it also finely.

Melt the butter, and gently *sauté* the vegetables in it for five minutes, taking care they do not discolour.

Boil the stock in another saucepan, and, when boiling, pour it on to the vegetables.

Simmer gently until the vegetables are quite tender.

Beat the yolks of the eggs with the cream, and when the stock has cooled a little strain them through a hair sieve into it.

Put the stewpan by the fire, and stir until the eggs thicken, taking care that the stock does not boil, as that would curdle them.

Add pepper and salt to taste, and the soup is ready.

The crust of the French roll should be served in the soup; it should be baked in the oven and then cut into fancy shapes.

Turnip Soup.

Ingredients—1 quart of stock, or the boilings from mutton.

2 lb. of turnips.

1 large onion.

½ pint of cream, or good milk.

2 large slices of bread.

Pepper and salt to taste.

Method.—Put the bread to soak in a little cold stock.

Pare the turnips and onions, and cut them in pieces.

Boil them gently in the stock, adding (when well soaked) the bread.

When the turnips are cooked, rub the soup through a wire sieve.

Put it again into the saucepan.

Add to it the cream or milk, pepper and salt to taste; and let it well boil up.

Serve with fried or toasted *croutons* of bread.

Rabbit Soup.

Ingredients—1 large rabbit.

2 quarts of water.

½ pint of milk or cream.

2 good-sized onions.

Method.—Cut the rabbit into joints.

Put them in a stewpan with the onions sliced and the water.

Stew very gently for three hours.

Then strain the stock and remove the fat.

Put it into a clean stewpan and add a thickening of flour, taking one ounce of flour to every pint of soup.

Stir and cook well.

Add the milk or cream and boil it in the soup.

Season with pepper and salt to taste, and serve with fried or toasted bread.

It is an improvement to this soup to cook a ham-bone with the rabbit, or a slice of lean pork.

Hare Soup.

Ingredients—1 hare.

1 lb. of gravy beef.

1 carrot, 1 turnip, and 1 onion.

1 sprig of parsley, thyme, and marjoram.

1 bay leaf.

1 dozen peppercorns.

1 blade of mace and 5 cloves.

2 or 3 oz. of butter or dripping.

7 pints of water.

Method.—Cut the hare into joints, and the meat into pieces, and fry them in a stewpan in the butter or dripping.

Afterwards fry the vegetables in the same fat.

Then pour in the water, add the mace and pepper-corns, and simmer gently from four to five hours.

Strain the stock and let it get cold.

Remove the fat perfectly, and put it into a clean stewpan on the fire.

When it boils stir in a thickening of flour, using one ounce of flour to every pint of soup.

Cook the flour well, and add a little colouring if necessary.

Season to taste, and, just before serving, pour in two glasses of port wine.

Some forcemeat balls should be served in the soup.

Make them with veal forcemeat, mixed with the liver of the hare finely chopped, and bake them in the oven.

Mulligatawny Soup.

Ingredients—1 rabbit or chicken.

2 quarts of second stock.

1 onion.

1 apple.

2 tablespoonfuls of curry powder.

½ pint of cream.

2 oz. of butter or dripping.

A few drops of lemon juice.

Method.—Cut the rabbit, or chicken, into joints, and fry them in the butter or dripping.

Remove them when nicely browned, and fry the apple and onion.

Then put the apple, onion, and meat into a stewpan, with the stock, which should be mixed with the curry powder.

Simmer very gently for an hour and a half, until the meat is tender.

Then remove the meat from the stock, and cut it into neat pieces, convenient for serving in the soup, removing all the bone.

Thicken the soup with flour, using about one ounce to every pint of stock.

Boil the flour well in the stock, and then rub the soup through a wire sieve.

Put it into a stewpan, add the cream, and let it boil in the soup.

Put in the pieces of meat; and, just before serving, add a squeeze of lemon juice.

Serve nicely boiled rice with this soup (*see* Rice for Curry).

Parsnip Soup.

Ingredients—2 quarts of stock.

2 lb. of parsnips.

If possible, ½ pint of cream.

Pepper and salt to taste.

Method.—Slice the parsnips and put them into boiling stock.

Simmer them for one hour, or more, until quite tender.

Then rub the soup through a wire sieve.

Add the cream to it, and pepper and salt to taste.

Put it into a clean stewpan.

Boil up once more and it is ready.

Serve with fried *croutons* of bread.

Red Lentil Soup.

Ingredients—1 pint of Egyptian lentils.

1 large carrot.

3 onions.

2 lb. of parsnips.

1 sprig of parsley.

2 or 3 large crusts of bread.

2 quarts of water.

Pepper and salt to taste.

Method.—Wash the lentils well.

Boil with the vegetables, cut in slices, and the bread, for two hours or more; stirring occasionally when the lentils are nearly cooked, as they are apt to stick to the bottom of the saucepan and burn.

Rub the soup through a wire sieve, adding pepper and salt to taste.

Make it hot again, stirring all the time, and it is ready to serve.

Mock-Turtle Soup.

Ingredients—Half a calf's head.

3 oz. of butter.

1 shalot.

Half-a-dozen mushrooms.

1 carrot.

½ a head of celery.

1 leek.

1 onion.

1 small turnip.

1 sprig of parsley, thyme, and marjoram.

1 bay leaf.

1 blade of mace.

5 cloves.

3 oz. of flour.

2 wineglasses of sherry.

1 dozen forcemeat balls.

4 quarts of water.

¼ lb. of ham.

Pepper and salt to taste.

Method.—Wash the calf's head thoroughly.

Cut all the flesh from the bones and tie it in a cloth.

Put it, with the bones and water, into a large saucepan and let it simmer gently, stirring occasionally for three and a half hours.

Then take out the calf's head and strain the stock into a clean pan.

Let it get cold, and then carefully remove all the fat.

Then put the butter into a stewpan, and fry in it the ham and vegetables, cut into slices, with the herbs, mace, cloves, &c.

When they are fried, put in the flour and fry till a light brown, stirring it to keep it from burning.

Then pour in the stock and stir until it boils.

Add pepper and salt to taste; put it by the side of the fire to simmer for half an hour.

Remove all scum, or fat, as it rises.

Then strain the stock into another stewpan.

Cut part of the calf's head into neat pieces and add it to the stock.

Pour in the sherry and lemon juice, and add the forcemeat balls.

Let the soup just come to the boil, and it is ready for serving. The forcemeat balls should be made of veal stuffing, and should be either fried or baked.

They should not be too large.

It is better to make this soup the day before it is wanted.

Pot-au-Feu.

Ingredients—4 lb. of sticking of beef, or 4 lb. of ox cheek without the bone.

2 large carrots.

1 head of celery.

3 onions.

2 turnips.

3 sprigs of parsley, thyme, and marjoram.

3 cloves.

6 quarts of water.

2 oz. of crushed tapioca, or sago.

Pepper and salt to taste.

Method.—Tie the meat firmly into shape with string.

Put it into a large saucepan with the water.

When it boils, add a teaspoonful of salt.

Simmer the meat gently for nearly two hours.

Clean the vegetables thoroughly, tying the celery, parsnips, and carrots together.

Add them, with the exception of the cabbage, to the meat, and simmer gently for two hours more.

Then add the cabbage, cleaned and trimmed; it should be cut in two, and tied together with string.

Simmer until it is tender, adding pepper and salt to taste.

The meat is then served with the carrots, turnips, and parsnips, as a garnish, and a little of the liquor poured round for gravy.

The cabbage is served in a vegetable dish.

To make the soup, put two quarts of the liquor into a saucepan. When it boils sprinkle in the sago, or tapioca, and cook for fifteen minutes, stirring occasionally.

Dr. Kitchener's Broth.

Ingredients—4 oz. of Scotch barley.

4 oz. of sliced onions.

2 oz. of dripping.

3 oz. bacon.

4 oz. oatmeal.

5 quarts of the liquor from meat.

Method.—Wash the barley, and soak it in water for two hours.

Put the meat liquor on to boil.

When boiling, add the barley and the onions.

Let it boil gently for an hour and a half.

Then put the dripping into another saucepan, and fry the bacon in it.

Then add, by degrees, the oatmeal; stir until it forms a paste.

Then pour in the broth.

Season with pepper and salt to taste, and set it by the side of the fire to simmer for thirty minutes; the soup is then ready.

Crowdie.

Ingredients—1 gallon of liquor from meat.

¼ pint of oatmeal.

1 onion.

Pepper and salt.

Method.—Put the liquor into a saucepan on the fire.

Mix the oatmeal to a paste with cold water.

Pour it into the liquor when boiling.

Stir until it thickens.

Add the onion, finely-chopped, and pepper and salt to taste.

BREAD AND CAKES.

IN making bread be careful that the yeast is good; otherwise the bread may be heavy. The German and French yeast will do quite as well as the brewers', and are generally more easily procured. The French yeast is the closest and strongest, but, though less is required, bread made with it will take longer to rise than that made with German. The yeast may be tested by mixing it with a little sugar; if it is good, it has the power of dissolving the sugar to a syrup. Everything made with yeast should be allowed a proper time to rise. A quartern loaf will generally be ready to make up in about two hours after the dough is set, but the time of rising will vary according to circumstances—for example, in cold weather it may not rise so quickly as in hot. For making bread, warm the pan or tub the dough is to be mixed in, but do not make it hot. Take care that the flour is dry, and free from lumps. The water used must be warmed, but care must be taken that it is neither too hot nor too cold. A certain amount of warmth is necessary for the growth of the yeast, but too great heat kills it. The water, therefore, should be lukewarm. When the dough is mixed, sprinkle the top with a little flour to prevent a crust forming; the pan should then be covered with a cloth and placed on a chair in a warm place, free from draught. It may be placed with advantage before the oven or boiler, but should not be put directly in front of a fire. When the dough is exposed to too great a heat it gets moist and sticky, is very difficult to make up, and is heavy when baked. When the dough has risen sufficiently, it should be well kneaded, and then made up into loaves. These loaves are then set on floured tins to rise in a warm place for about twenty minutes before they are baked. The oven should be very hot for the first twenty minutes, and then very much moderated: a sharp heat is necessary at first to throw up the bread; but the rest of the time the heat applied should be moderate. The same heat is required in baking cakes: a sharp heat at first, to throw them up, and moderate afterwards, so that they may get cooked through without the crust burning. The sugar in cakes causes them to burn very quickly. It is, therefore, a wise precaution to line the tin, even for a plain cake, with foolscap paper.

Currants used in cakes should be well washed and dried before they are used, and any stones removed from them. Sultanas should be rubbed in flour, and the stalks picked off. Raisins should be stoned, and cut in two or three pieces.

To cream butter is to work it about in a basin with the hand, or wooden spoon, until it is the consistency of cream.

The cake tins should be kept in a dry place, and before using should be well greased, especially at the bottom.

A Quartern Loaf.

Ingredients—3½ lb. of flour.

1¾ pint of water.

½ oz. of salt.

1 oz. of German yeast.

Method.—Put 3 lb. of flour into the pan.

Make the water lukewarm, and mix it with the yeast.

Make a hole in the middle of the flour, and mix in the water smoothly and gradually.

Knead lightly for a minute or two.

Sprinkle with a little flour, and set to rise in a warm place for about two hours.

Then knead well for about a quarter of an hour, working in the remainder of the flour.

Make it into a loaf, and put it in or on a floured tin.

Set it to rise for about twenty minutes, and then bake.

The oven must be very hot for the first few minutes, and then the heat must be *much* lowered, that the bread may get well cooked through.

Vienna Bread.

Ingredients—2 lb. of Vienna flour.

2 oz. of butter.

1 oz. of German yeast.

1 pint of milk.

1 teaspoonful of salt.

Method.—Rub the butter well into the flour, and add the salt.

Make the milk tepid, and mix smoothly with the German yeast.

Make a well in the middle of the flour, and stir in the milk smoothly.

Knead very lightly for a minute, and then put the dough to rise in a warm place for two hours.

When it has well risen, make it into rolls or fancy twists.

Set them to rise on floured tins for about ten minutes.

Then bake in a quick oven from ten to twenty minutes, according to their size.

When nearly cooked, brush them with a little milk or white of egg to glaze them.

Unfermented Bread.

Ingredients—1 lb. of flour.

2 heaped teaspoonfuls of baking powder.

Enough water to mix a dough.

Method.—Put the flour in a pan.

Add the baking powder and mix up with the water.

Make it into small loaves quickly, and bake in a quick oven for about half an hour.

Milk Rolls.

Ingredients—1 lb. of flour.

2 oz. of butter.

2 heaped teaspoonfuls of baking powder.

Enough milk to mix to a dough.

Method.—Rub the butter into the flour lightly.

Add the baking powder, and mix with the milk.

Make into small rolls as quickly as possible, and bake for a few minutes in a quick oven.

Brush over with a little milk to glaze them.

Pound Cake.

Ingredients—10 oz. of flour.

8 oz. of butter.

8 oz. of castor sugar.

2 oz. of candied peel.

¼ lb. of sultanas.

4 large eggs.

Grated rind of a lemon.

Method.—Rub the flour and sugar through a sieve.

Beat the butter to a cream in a basin.

Mix in a little flour and sugar.

Then a well-beaten egg.

Next more flour, sugar, and another egg.

Continue mixing in the same way until the flour, sugar, and eggs are all well blended together.

Add the other ingredients, and put into a well-greased cake-tin lined with buttered paper.

Bake for about two hours.

Queen Cakes.

Ingredients—6 oz. of flour.

4 oz. of butter.

4 oz. of sugar.

4 eggs.

A few currants.

Grated rind of a lemon.

Method.—Cream the butter.

Mix in the flour, sugar, and eggs, according to directions given in preceding recipe.

Add the lemon rind, and partly fill small well-greased Queen-cake tins with the mixture.

Sprinkle a few currants on the top of each.

Bake in a moderately quick oven for about a quarter of an hour.

Rock Cakes.

Ingredients—1 lb. of flour.

6 oz. of butter.

6 oz. of castor sugar.

½ lb. of currants.

2 oz. of candied peel.

1 teaspoonful of baking powder.

2 eggs.

Grated rind of a lemon.

Method.—Rub the butter into the flour.

Add the sugar, currants, and other ingredients.

Mix very stiffly with the eggs, well beaten.

Put in rough heaps on a well-greased baking-sheet.

Bake in a quick oven for a quarter of an hour.

Plain Rock Cakes.

Ingredients—1 lb. of flour.

¼ lb. of moist sugar.

¼ lb. of currants.

¼ lb. of butter, lard, or dripping.

1 egg.

A little milk.

Method.—Rub the butter or dripping into the flour.

Add the other dry ingredients.

Mix stiffly with the egg, well beaten, and a little milk.

Put in little rough heaps on a well-greased baking-tin.

Bake in a quick oven for about a quarter of an hour.

Plain Seed Cake.

Ingredients—10 oz. of flour.

3 oz. of butter or clarified dripping.

1 teaspoonful of caraway seeds.

3 oz. of castor sugar.

2 teaspoonfuls of baking powder.

1 egg.

¾ gill of milk.

½ saltspoonful of salt.

Method.—Rub the fat well into the flour.

Add all the other dry ingredients.

Mix with the egg and milk, well beaten.

Bake in a well-greased cake-tin for about an hour.

Sultana Cake.

Ingredients—10 oz. of flour.

¼ lb. butter.

¼ lb. of castor sugar.

¼ lb. of sultana raisins.

1 oz. of candied peel.

2 eggs.

1 teaspoonful of baking powder.

½ gill of milk.

Grated rind of a lemon.

Method.—Rub the butter well into the flour.

Add all the other dry ingredients.

Mix with the milk and yolks of the eggs, well beaten together.

Beat the whites of the eggs to a stiff froth, and mix them in lightly.

Put the mixture in a well-greased cake-tin.

Bake for about one hour and a half.

Plain Plum Cake.

Ingredients—1 lb. of flour.

¼ lb. of dripping.

¼ lb. of currants.

½ pint of milk.

¼ lb. of sugar.

2 teaspoonfuls of baking powder.

Method.—Rub the dripping into the flour.

Add the other dry ingredients.

Mix with the milk.

Bake in a well-greased cake-tin for about one hour and a quarter.

Rice Cake.

Ingredients—8 oz. of ground rice.

6 oz. of castor sugar.

4 eggs.

Grated rind of a lemon.

Method.—Beat the eggs well with a whisk.

Mix in gradually the castor sugar and rice, and add the lemon rind.

Bake in a well-greased baking-tin in a quick oven for about one hour.

Cornflour Cake.

Ingredients—¼ lb. of cornflour.

¼ lb. of castor sugar.

2 oz. of butter.

1 teaspoonful of baking powder.

2 eggs.

Method.—Beat the butter to a cream.

Then mix in the sugar.

Add the two eggs, and beat all well together.

Lastly, stir in the cornflour and add the baking powder.

Put the mixture into a well-greased cake-tin, and bake for about three-quarters of an hour.

Scones.

Ingredients—1 lb. of flour.

2 oz. of castor sugar.

3 oz. of butter.

½ pint of milk.

2 teaspoonfuls of baking powder, or ¼ oz. of cream of tartar, and

1 teaspoonful of carbonate of soda.

Method.—Rub the butter into the flour.

Add the other dry ingredients.

Mix lightly with the milk.

Divide the dough into two pieces.

Make each piece into a ball.

Roll it out to about three-quarters of an inch in thickness.

Cut into triangular-shaped pieces.

Bake on a greased baking-tin for about twenty minutes.

Brush them over with a little white of egg or milk to glaze them.

Currant Cake.

Ingredients—10 oz. of flour.

¼ lb. of currants.

¼ lb. of sugar.

3 oz. of butter.

1 egg.

2 teaspoonfuls of baking powder.

¼ pint of milk.

A little grated lemon rind.

Method.—Rub the butter into the flour until like fine bread-crumbs.

Add the sugar and currants—the currants should be well washed and dried—also the baking powder and lemon rind.

Mix with the beaten egg and milk.

Bake it at once, in a greased cake-tin lined with paper, for one hour and a half.

Luncheon Cake.

Ingredients—1 lb. of flour.

4 oz. of butter, lard, or dripping.
¼ lb. of sultanas.
¼ lb. of currants.
6 oz. of sugar.
2 oz. of candied peel.
2 eggs.
Rather less than a ¼ pint of milk.
2 teaspoonfuls of baking powder.
1 oz. of lump sugar.
Grated lemon rind.

Method.—Put the lump sugar in a saucepan and burn it brown.
Pour in the milk and stir until it is coloured.
Then strain it and let it get cold.
Put the flour into a basin.
Rub the butter lightly into it.
Add the sultanas (well cleaned), and the rest of the dry ingredients.
Mix with the eggs well beaten, and the milk.
Put it into a well-greased tin, which should be lined with paper.
Bake from one hour and a half to two hours.

Gingerbread.

Ingredients—2 lb. of flour.
2 lb. of treacle.
½ lb. moist sugar.
3 eggs.
½ oz. of carbonate of soda.
8 oz. of butter.
2 oz. of ginger.

½ a cup of water.

2 oz. of candied peel.

Method.—Put the flour, sugar, ginger, candied peel, and carbonate of soda into a basin.

Warm the treacle, water, and butter in a saucepan.

Mix with the dry ingredients and add the eggs, well beaten.

Partly fill a well-greased Yorkshire-pudding tin.

Smooth over with a knife dipped in hot water, and score with a knife.

Bake in a moderate oven for about an hour and a half.

Sponge Cake.

Ingredients—4 oz. of flour.

5 eggs.

4 oz. of castor sugar.

Method.—Oil the cake-mould, and dust it over with castor sugar.

Beat the eggs and sugar for about twenty minutes until they rise and are quite light; this may be done over hot water, care being taken that the heat is not too great to cook the eggs.

Dry and sift the flour, and stir it lightly in.

Pour into the mould and bake in a moderate oven for about one hour.

Sponge Roll.

Ingredients—5 eggs.

The weight of 4 eggs in castor sugar.

Of 3 in flour.

Some jam.

Method.—Beat the eggs to a cream.

Add the sugar and then the flour, lightly.

Have a baking-tin ready greased with butter, and lined with greased paper.

Pour in the mixture; spread it over and bake it till a light fawn colour.

Then turn it on to a cloth.

Spread with the jam melted and roll up quickly.

Seed Cake.

Ingredients—1 lb. of flour.

4 oz. of butter.

6 oz. of castor sugar.

½ oz. of caraway seeds.

¼ pint of milk.

1 teaspoonful of baking powder.

2 eggs.

Method.—Rub the butter into the flour.

Add the castor sugar and seeds.

Mix with the yolks and milk beaten together.

Beat the whites stiffly and stir in lightly.

Bake in a nicely prepared tin for about one hour and a half.

Madeira Cake.

Ingredients—10 oz. of flour.

10 oz. of lump sugar.

¼ lb. of butter.

6 eggs.

½ gill of water.

Method.—Boil the water and sugar to a syrup.

Pour when hot, but not boiling, on to the eggs and beat over hot water until light.

Melt the butter and stir it in very lightly with the flour.

Oil a mould and dust it with castor sugar.

Pour in the mixture, and bake from one hour and a half to two hours.

Buns.

Ingredients—16 oz. of flour.

½ oz. of yeast.

½ pint of milk.

2 oz. of sugar.

2 oz. of sultanas.

2 oz. of butter.

1 egg.

Method.—Put ten ounces of the flour into a basin.

Mix the yeast smoothly with the milk, which should be made tepid.

Stir into the flour.

Beat for five minutes, and set to rise in a warm place for about two hours.

Then beat in the remainder of the flour, sultanas, sugar, butter, and the egg.

Set to rise for about two hours more.

Then form into buns.

Place them on a floured tin, and let them rise for ten minutes.

Bake in a very quick oven for about five minutes until nicely coloured.

Boil half an ounce of sugar with half a gill of water, and brush the buns over with this to glaze them.

Dough Cake.

Ingredients—½ quartern of dough.

¼ lb. of currants.

¼ lb. of moist sugar.

¼ lb. of clarified dripping.

Method.—Put the dough into a basin.

Beat in the dripping, sugar, and currants.

These should be well washed and dried.

Place in a greased tin, and set to rise for one hour.

Bake in a moderate oven for two hours.

Candied-peel Drops.

Ingredients—½ lb. of flour.

3 oz. of butter.

3 oz. of candied peel.

Grated rind of a lemon.

1 egg.

A little milk.

One teaspoonful of baking powder.

3 oz. of sugar.

Method.—Rub the butter into the flour.

Add the sugar, grated lemon rind, baking powder, and the candied peel chopped small.

Mix with the egg, well beaten, and the milk.

Put it in little heaps on a greased baking-tin.

Bake in a quick oven for about fifteen minutes.

Shrewsbury Cakes.

Ingredients—¼ lb. of butter.

¼ lb. of castor sugar.

6 oz. of flour.

1 egg.

Method.—Cream the butter and sugar.

Add to them the egg, well beaten.

Then stir in the flour.

Knead it to a dough.

Roll out, and cut into small round cakes with a cutter.

Place them on a greased baking-sheet.

Bake in a moderate oven from fifteen to twenty minutes.

Oatmeal Biscuits.

Ingredients—7 oz. of flour.

3 oz. of oatmeal.

3 oz. of castor sugar.

3 oz. of lard, dripping, or butter.

¼ teaspoonful of baking powder.

1 egg.

1 tablespoonful of water.

Method.—Put the flour, oatmeal, sugar, and baking-powder into a basin.

Mix them with the fat melted, and the egg beaten with the water.

Knead lightly into a dough.

Roll it out, and cut into round cakes.

Place them on a greased baking-tin.

Bake in a moderate oven for about twenty minutes.

Shortbread.

Ingredients—¼ lb. of flour.

1 oz. of castor sugar.

2 oz. of butter.

Method.—Put the flour and sugar into a basin.

Melt the butter, and mix them with it.

Knead lightly.

Roll out, cut the paste into cakes with a knife, and bake for half an hour.

Yorkshire Teacakes.

Ingredients—¾ lb. of flour.

1½ gill of milk.

1 oz. of butter.

1 egg.

½ oz. of German yeast.

Method.—Put the flour into a basin, and rub the butter into it.

Make the milk tepid, and blend it with the yeast.

Strain it into the flour.

Add the egg.

Beat all well together for a few minutes.

Knead lightly.

Then divide the dough in two.

Make each part into a ball, and put them in floured cake-tins.

Put the cakes in a warm place to rise for one hour, and then bake them for about twenty minutes.

Brush them over with a syrup of sugar and water to glaze them.

Ginger Biscuits.

Ingredients—½ lb. of flour.

2 oz. of butter, lard, or dripping.

½ oz. of ground ginger.

2 oz. of castor sugar.

1 egg, and a little milk.

½ teaspoonful of baking powder.

Method.—Rub the butter into the flour until it is like fine bread-crumbs.

Add the sugar and baking powder, and mix with the egg, well beaten, and as much milk as necessary to make it bind.

Roll out, and cut into small round cakes.

Put them on a greased tin.

Bake in a moderate oven for about twenty minutes.

Lemon-rock Cakes.

Ingredients—1 lb. of flour.

3 oz. of butter.

5 oz. of castor sugar.

Grated rind of one lemon and juice of two.

1 egg.

A little milk.

1 teaspoonful of baking powder.

Method.—Rub the butter into the flour.

Add the sugar, baking-powder, lemon rind, and juice.

Mix with the egg, well beaten, and as much milk as necessary; the mixture should be very stiff.

Put it in little rough heaps on a greased baking-tin.

Bake in a quick oven for about fifteen minutes.

Soda Cakes.

Ingredients—½ lb. of flour.

2 oz. of butter.

3 oz. of sugar.

1 oz. of candied peel.

Grated rind of a lemon.

1 whole egg.

If necessary, a little milk.

½ a teaspoonful of carbonate soda.

Method.—Rub the butter well into the flour.

Add the sugar, peel, lemon rind, and soda.

Mix with the egg, well beaten, and, if necessary, a little milk; the mixture must be very stiff.

Put it in little rough heaps on a greased baking-tin.

Bake in a quick oven for fifteen minutes.

Gingerbread Cakes.

Ingredients—1 lb. of flour.

6 oz. of butter, lard, or dripping.

1 oz. of ground ginger.

4 oz. of moist sugar.

¾ lb. of treacle.

Method.—Put the sugar, treacle, and fat into a saucepan, and melt them.

Put the flour and ginger into a basin.

Mix with the other ingredients.

Roll out, and cut into small cakes.

Bake on a greased baking-tin, in a slow oven, for ten or fifteen minutes.

Rice Buns.

Ingredients—¼ lb. of ground rice.

¼ lb. of castor sugar.

2 oz. of butter.

1 egg.

½ a teaspoonful of baking powder.

A little flavouring essence.

Method.—Beat the butter to a cream with the sugar.

Then add the eggs, well beaten, and stir in the ground rice.

Partly fill little greased patty-pans with the mixture, and bake in a moderate oven for a quarter of an hour.

Galettes.

Ingredients—1 lb. of Vienna flour.

1 lb. of household flour.

1 oz. of yeast.

½ lb. of butter.

6 eggs.

½ a pint of milk.

A little sugar.

Method.—Make the milk tepid.

Then mix it smoothly with the yeast, and stir it into the household flour.

Knead it to a dough.

Rub the butter into the other flour and beat in the eggs well with the sugar.

Then knead both doughs together.

Put them to rise for about two hours.

When nicely risen, make the dough into buns.

Put them on a floured baking-sheet.

Bake in a quick oven for about ten minutes.

When nearly ready, brush over with a little white of egg to glaze them.

JELLIES AND CREAMS.

To clear Jellies.

TAKE a large saucepan, and see that it is perfectly clean. Put into it all the ingredients for the jelly, and the whites and shells of the eggs. The use of the whites of eggs is to clear the jelly; the shells form a filter through which to strain it. Whisk all together over a quick fire until the jelly begins to simmer; then immediately leave off stirring, and let it well boil up. The heat of the boiling jelly hardens the egg, which rises to the surface in the form of a thick scum, bringing all impurities with it. If the stirring were continued during the boiling it would prevent the scum rising properly, and the jelly would not clear.

When the jelly has well boiled up, remove it from the fire and let it stand for a few minutes till a crust is formed.

To strain it, a chair may be turned upside down, and a cloth tied firmly to its four legs. Any cloth, which is clean, and not too closely woven, will answer the purpose. Put a basin under the cloth, and pour some boiling water through it. This will make it hot, and ensure its being perfectly clean. Change the basin for a clean dry one, and pour the whole contents of the saucepan on to the cloth. The first runnings of the jelly will be cloudy, because the filter which the eggs make will not have settled in the cloth. As soon as the jelly runs slowly, and looks clear, put a clean basin under the cloth, and put the first runnings through it again, very gently, that they may not disturb the filter of egg-shells.

Strain the jelly in a warm place, out of draught. Two eggs are considered sufficient to clarify a quart of jelly, but if the eggs are small it is wise to take a third. If there is not sufficient white of egg, the jelly will not clear.

The jelly should be allowed to get nearly cold before it is put into the moulds. If it is put hot into metal moulds it is likely to become cloudy.

To make Creams.

To make a good cream, it is essential that the cream used should be double; that is, a thick cream that will whip up to a stiff froth. Beat it well with a wire whisk until it will stand on the end of it without dropping. This must be done in a cool place, especially in summer time. Cream is liable to curdle, and turn to butter, if beaten in too warm a temperature. The gelatine must be added last of all. It should be stirred in thoroughly, but quickly; it must not be too hot, or too cold, but just lukewarm. If too hot, it destroys the lightness of the cream; if too cold, it does not mix thoroughly. Pour the cream into a mould as soon as the gelatine is mixed with it, as it begins to set directly. To turn a jelly or cream out of its mould, take a basin of hot water, as hot as the hand can bear, draw the mould quickly through it, letting the water quite cover it for a second. Wipe off all the moisture immediately with a dry cloth. Shake the tin gently, to be sure the contents are free. Lay the dish on the open side of the mould, quickly reverse it, and draw the mould carefully away.

Strawberry Cream.

Ingredients—½ pint of double cream.

1 oz. of amber gelatine, or rather less than ½ oz. of the opaque.

2 tablespoonfuls of castor sugar.

Some strawberries.

¼ pint of milk.

A few drops of cochineal.

Method.—Soak the gelatine in the milk for about twenty minutes or more.

Then dissolve it by stirring it in a saucepan over the fire.

Rub sufficient strawberries through a hair sieve to make a quarter of a pint of *purée*.

Beat up the cream with the sugar.

Then add the *purée* of fruit, and a few drops of cochineal to colour it.

Lastly stir in the melted gelatine.

Pour the cream at once into a wetted mould.

When quite set, dip it for a second or two into very hot water, and turn it on to a glass dish.

Charlotte Russe.

Ingredients—1 dozen sponge fingers.

1 oz. of glace cherries.

½ pint of double cream.

½ oz. of amber gelatine melted in a little milk, or less than ¼ oz. of the opaque.

2 dessertspoonfuls of castor sugar.

A few drops of essence of vanilla, or other flavouring.

Method.—First put the gelatine to soak in a little milk.

Then cut the cherries in halves, and place them in a circle round the bottom of a plain round tin, with the cut side uppermost.

Divide the sponge fingers, lengthwise, without breaking them, and trim each one at the side, top, and bottom neatly.

Then line the tin with them, placing them on the top of the cherries, with the brown side next the tin; they should be put close together, and the last should serve as a wedge to keep the others in place.

Beat up the cream stiffly with the sugar.

Add the vanilla flavouring and the melted gelatine. This must be neither too hot nor too cold.

Stir it thoroughly, but quickly, into the cream, and pour at once into the prepared tin.

When set, dip the bottom of the tin into hot water for a second or two, and turn it carefully on to a glass dish.

Custard Cream.

Ingredients—½ pint of double cream.

3 tablespoonfuls of castor sugar.

1 oz. of amber gelatine, or less than ½ of the opaque.

1 whole egg.

3 yolks.

½ pint of hot milk.

A few drops of vanilla or other essence.

Method.—Put the gelatine to soak in a little milk.

Then beat the eggs lightly and add them to the milk.

Strain into a jug and add the sugar.

Put the jug into a saucepan of boiling water, and stir until the custard coats the spoon; care must be taken that it does not curdle.

While the custard cools beat up the cream stiffly.

Melt the gelatine, and add it to the custard.

Flavour it, and, when sufficiently cooled, mix the custard and cream thoroughly together.

Pour at once into a wetted mould.

Bohemian Cream.

Ingredients—½ pint of sweet jelly of any kind.

½ pint of double cream.

Method.—Beat the cream stiffly.

Mix with it the jelly, which should be melted, but cold.

Pour into a wetted mould.

Wine Jelly.

Ingredients—1 oz. packet of either Nelson's or Swinbourne's gelatine.

1 pint of water.

½ pint of sherry.

¼ to ½ lb. of lump sugar, according to taste.

The juice of two lemons.

The rind of one.

The whites and shells of 2 large eggs.

Method.—Soak the gelatine in the water with the thin rind of a lemon for three quarters of an hour, if possible.

Then add all the other ingredients.

Clarify and strain (*see* To clear Jellies).

When quite cold pour into a wetted mould.

Calf's-foot Stock.

Ingredients—2 calf's feet.

4 pints of water.

Method.—Cut each foot into four pieces.

Blanch them by putting them in cold water and bringing them to the boil.

Throw the water away, and well wash the feet.

Put them into a saucepan, with four pints of water, and boil gently for five hours.

Then strain the stock from the bones, and set it aside until the next day.

The fat must then be carefully removed, or the stock will not clear.

To turn this into Calf's-foot Jelly, add—

>Half a pint of white wine.
>The rind of 2 and the juice of 4 lemons.

¾ lb. of lump sugar.

The whites and shells of 4 eggs.

Clarify and strain (*see* To clear Jellies).

Pineapple Jelly.

Ingredients—1 pineapple.

1 oz. packet of gelatine.

1 pint of water.

¼ lb. of lump sugar.

The thin rind of 1 lemon, and the juice of 2.

The whites and shells of 2 large eggs.

Method.—First soak the gelatine in the water.

Cut up the pineapple and bruise it in a mortar.

Add it, and all the other ingredients, to the gelatine.

Then clarify (*see* To clear Jellies).

Note.—The Grated Pineapple, sold in tins, is excellent for jellies or creams.

Aspic Jelly.

Ingredients—1 oz. packet of gelatine.

1 pint of good stock.

¼ pint of taragon vinegar.

¼ pint of sherry.

A small carrot, turnip, and onion.

A sprig of parsley, thyme, and marjoram.

2 bay leaves.

3 cloves.

1 dozen peppercorns.

A piece of celery.

A blade of mace.

A clove of garlic.

1 shalot.

The whites and shells of 2 large eggs.

Salt to taste.

Method.—Soak the gelatine in the stock.

Then add all the other ingredients and clarify (*see* To clear Jellies).

Claret Jelly.

Ingredients—1 oz. packet of gelatine.

½ pint of water.

1 pint of claret.

½ lb. of lump sugar.

A few drops of cochineal.

Method.—Soak the gelatine in the water.

Add the sugar, and stir over the fire until dissolved.

Pour in the wine, and colour with cochineal.

Strain into a wetted mould.

When firm, dip into hot water for a second or two, and turn on to a glass dish.

Note.—This jelly is not clarified. Cake is usually served with claret jelly.

Orange Jelly.

Ingredients—1 dozen oranges.

1 lemon.

2 pints of water.

1 oz. packet and a half of Swinbourne's or Nelson's opaque gelatine (in summer two packets).

½ lb. of lump sugar.

Method.—Soak the gelatine in the water with the thin rind of one lemon and three oranges.

Add the sugar; stir over the fire until the gelatine is dissolved.

Add the juice of the twelve oranges.

Let the jelly boil up, and then strain into a wetted mould.

When firm, dip into hot water for a second or two, and turn on to a glass dish.

NOTE.—This jelly is not clarified.

Strawberry Jelly.

Ingredients—1 quart of strawberries.

½ lb. of lump sugar.

Juice of one lemon.

1½ oz. of Swinbourne's or Nelson's opaque gelatine.

½ pint of cold water.

½ pint of boiling water.

The whites and shells of 2 large eggs.

Method.—Soak the gelatine in the cold water.

Mash the strawberries to a pulp.

Add them to the gelatine with the sugar and lemon juice.

Pour the boiling water over.

Then put all the ingredients into a saucepan.

Add to them the whites and shells of the eggs, and clarify and strain (*see* To clear Jellies).

Pour into a wetted mould, and set in a cool place until firm.

To turn it out, dip the tin into very hot water for a second or two, and turn it carefully on to a glass dish.

Orange Cream.

Ingredients—1 pint of double cream.

4 oranges.

4 oz. of sugar.

1 oz. packet of gelatine.

2 whole eggs.

Yolks of 4 eggs.

1 pint of milk.

Method.—Soak the gelatine in a ¼ pint of milk with the thin rind of one orange.

Strain the juice of the oranges into a cup.

Beat the eggs, and yolks of eggs, with the milk.

Strain into a jug, and add the sugar.

Put the jug to stand in a saucepan of boiling water, and stir until the custard coats the spoon.

Melt the gelatine and add it to the custard.

Whip up the cream stiffly, and add to it the orange juice.

When the custard is cool, beat it into the cream, and pour at once into a wetted mould.

If liked, it may be put into a border mould, and served with whipped cream in the middle.

Blancmange.

Ingredients—1 oz. packet of Swinbourne's isinglass.

1 pint of milk.

1 pint of cream.

3 or 4 oz. castor sugar.

Flavouring essence.

Method.—Soak the isinglass in the milk; add the sugar and stir over the fire until both are dissolved.

Then pour in the cream; stir occasionally until cold.

Add the flavouring essence and pour it into a wetted mould.

NOTE.—A *blancmange* may be made economically by using less cream and more milk, or using milk only. If it is not stirred until cold, the cream and milk will separate.

Vanilla Cream.

Make a thick cream as for Charlotte Russe, and flavour with vanilla.

Gâteau aux Pommes.

Ingredients—2 lb. apples.

3 oz. moist sugar.

1 lemon.

½ oz. packet of Swinbourne's or Nelson's gelatine.

½ pint of water.

A few drops of cochineal.

Method.—Soak the gelatine in half the water.

Wash and slice the apples.

Put them in a stewpan with the sugar and thin lemon rind and juice and remainder of the water.

Stew until soft, then rub through a *hair* sieve.

Melt the gelatine; mix it thoroughly with the apples.

Colour with cochineal, and pour the mixture into a wetted mould.

NOTE.—This sweet looks very nice when it is made in a border mould. It is then served with whipped cream or white of egg in the middle.

Peaches, prunes, or any suitable fruit may be substituted for the apples.

Compote of Peaches.

Ingredients—10 oz. of sugar.

1 pint of water.

1 dozen peaches.

½ pint of whipped cream.

Method.—Boil the sugar and water for ten minutes.

Pare the peaches and simmer for about twenty minutes.

Remove carefully and place on a glass dish.

Reduce the syrup and pour over them.

When cold, cover with whipped cream.

Almond Bavarian Cream.

Ingredients—1 pint of double cream.

½ lb. of sweet almonds.

1 or 2 drops of essence of almonds.

4 oz. of castor sugar.

¾ of an ounce packet of gelatine.

3 eggs.

¾ of a pint of milk.

Method.—Soak the gelatine in the milk.

Blanch and pound the almonds, adding a few drops of orange-flower water to keep them from oiling.

Beat the eggs and milk lightly together, and strain into a jug.

Add to them the sugar and almonds.

Put the jug into a saucepan of boiling water, and stir until the custard coats the spoon.

Melt the gelatine, and add it to the custard.

Whip the cream to a stiff froth, and drop in the almond essence.

When the custard is cool, stir it into the cream.

Mix them well together, and pour into a wetted mould.

Stone Cream.

Ingredients—1 pint of double cream.

2 wineglasses of sherry.

Juice of a lemon.

¼ lb. of castor sugar.

1 gill of milk.

1 oz. of Nelson's or Swinbourne's opaque gelatine.

A little almond flavouring.

Method.—Soak the gelatine in the milk with the sugar.

Beat the cream up stiffly.

Melt the gelatine; add to it the sherry, lemon juice, and flavouring.

Stir it quickly into the beaten cream.

Pour it into a wetted mould.

When set, dip it into very hot water for a second, and turn it carefully on to a glass dish.

Lemon Sponge.

Ingredients—½ oz. packet of gelatine.

1 pint of cold water.

½ lb. of lump sugar.

The thin rind and juice of two lemons.

The whites of 3 eggs.

Method.—Soak the gelatine in the water with the rind of the lemon for one hour.

Add the sugar and dissolve it over the fire.

Stir and simmer it for a few minutes.

Strain into a basin and add the lemon juice.

When it begins to set, beat in the whites of the eggs, whipped to a very stiff froth.

Whisk until the whole mixture is light and spongy.

Then heap it on a glass dish.

A little of it may be coloured a pale pink with cochineal; and as a decoration, a few pistachio kernels, blanched and chopped, can be sprinkled over the sponge.

Floating Island.

Ingredients—A round sponge-cake.

1 pint of custard (*see* Boiled Custard).

Red jam.

The whites of two eggs.

1 tablespoonful of castor sugar.

Some chopped pistachio kernels.

Some hundreds and thousands.

Method.—Cut the cake horizontally in slices.

Spread them with jam.

Place them on each other in the form of the cake, and spread the top with jam.

Put the cake on a glass dish, and pour the custard over.

Whip the whites of the eggs stiffly with the sugar, and heap on the top of the cake.

Decorate with chopped pistachios and hundreds and thousands.

Maraschino Cream.

Ingredients—3 yolks of eggs.

1 white.

½ pint of milk.

½ pint of whipped double cream.

2 tablespoonfuls of castor sugar.

1 oz. of amber gelatine, or ½ oz. of the opaque, melted in a little milk.

1 small glass of maraschino.

Method.—Make the eggs and milk into a custard (*see* Boiled Custard).

Add to it the sugar and melted gelatine.

When it has cooled, mix it with the cream.

Add the maraschino and pour into a wetted mould previously decorated with a little bright fruit.

When set, dip into hot water for a second or two, and turn it on to a glass dish.

Pistachio Cream.

Ingredients—½ pint of whipped double cream.

½ oz. of amber gelatine, or less than ¼ oz. of the opaque, melted in a little milk.

1 oz. of castor sugar.

2 oz. of pistachio kernels blanched.

A few drops of vanilla.

Method.—Pound the pistachios in a mortar, and rub them through a sieve.

Then mix them with the cream.

Add a few drops of vanilla, the sugar, and, last of all, the melted gelatine.

Pour it into a wetted mould.

When set, dip it into hot water for a second or two, and turn carefully on to a glass dish.

Croquant of Oranges.

Ingredients—9 or 10 oranges.

½ teacupful of melted sweet jelly.

A few pistachio kernels, blanched and chopped.

½ pint of whipped double cream.

½ oz. of amber gelatine, or less than ¼ oz. of the opaque, melted in a little milk.

2 oz. of castor sugar.

Method.—Peel and divide six oranges into sections, and carefully remove the white skins.

Dip each piece into the jelly, and line a plain round charlotte Russe tin with them.

Place them to form a star in the bottom of the mould, and fill up any spaces with the chopped pistachio kernels.

Add the juice of three oranges to the whipped cream.

Mix in the sugar, and add, last of all, the melted gelatine.

Pour the cream into the tin.

When set, dip the tin in hot water to loosen the pieces of orange, and then turn carefully on to a glass or silver dish.

Chartreuse de Fruit.

Ingredients—Various fruits, such as strawberries, greengages, cherries, peaches, &c.

Some strawberry or other cream.

½ teacupful of sweet jelly, melted.

Method.—Line a plain charlotte Russe mould tastefully with slices of the different fruits, dipping each piece in the melted jelly.

Then pour in a strawberry or any other cream (*see* Strawberry Cream).

When set, dip the mould into very hot water for a second or two to loosen the fruit, and then turn them on to a glass or silver dish.

Strawberry Charlotte.

Ingredients—Some fine ripe strawberries.

Some pistachio kernels, blanched and chopped.

½ teacupful of melted sweet jelly.

Some strawberry cream.

Method.—Line a Charlotte Russe mould tastefully with the strawberries cut in half, dipping them in the jelly, and laying them in the tin with the cut side downwards.

Fill the spaces with the pistachios.

When the strawberries are quite firm, pour in some strawberry cream (*see* Strawberry Cream).

When set, dip into very hot water for a second or two to loosen the fruit, and turn on to a glass or silver dish.

Tipsy Cake.

Ingredients—1 large sponge cake.
1 wineglass of sherry.
1 wineglass of brandy.
1 pint custard (*see* Boiled Custard).
Some blanched almonds.

Method.—Put the cake on a glass dish.
Soak it with the sherry and brandy.
Pour over the custard, and stick blanched almonds well over it.

Trifle.

Ingredients—1 Savoy cake.
1 pint of double cream.
1 pint of rich custard (*see* Boiled Custard).
Some strawberry or other jam.
1 wineglass of sherry.
1 wineglass of brandy.
½ lb. of macaroons.
1 oz. of castor sugar.
6 sponge cakes.

Method.—Cut the cake into slices an inch thick.
Lay them on the bottom of a glass dish.
Spread them with jam.

Lay the macaroons on them.

Cover them with sponge cakes.

Soak them with the sherry and brandy, and cover with the custard.

Whip the cream very stiffly with the sugar.

Drain it on a sieve.

Before serving, heap the whip on the top of the trifle.

Decorate it with chopped pistachios, and hundreds and thousands.

Apple Flummery.

Ingredients—2 lb. of apples.

The rind and juice of a small lemon.

5 oz. of sugar.

¼ pint of water.

½ oz. packet of Nelson's or Swinbourn's gelatine.

½ pint of cream.

Cochineal.

Method.—Cut up the apples, and stew them with the sugar, lemon, and water, until tender.

Rub them through a hair sieve.

While the apples are cooking, soak the gelatine in the cream.

Then stir over the fire until the gelatine is quite dissolved.

Add the cream and gelatine to the apple pulp, and beat all well together.

Colour with cochineal, and pour into a wetted mould.

When firm, dip for a second or two into very hot water, and then turn on to a glass dish.

Apple Cream.

Ingredients—2 lb. of apples.

¼ lb. of sugar.

1 glass of port wine.

The rind of a lemon.

¼ pint of water.

½ pint of cream or milk.

Cochineal.

Method.—Wash the apples, and cut them into pieces.

Put them into a stewpan with the lemon rind, sugar, wine, and water.

Stew gently until they are quite tender.

Then rub them through a hair sieve, and colour with cochineal.

Boil the cream or milk and add it to the apple pulp.

Beat them thoroughly together, and serve when cold in a glass dish.

Alpine Snow.

Ingredients—1½ lb. of apples.

3 oz. of castor sugar.

¼ pint of water.

The thin rind and juice of half a lemon.

The whites of 3 eggs.

Cochineal.

Method.—Wash the apples and cut them in pieces.

Put them in a stewpan with the water, sugar, lemon rind and juice.

Stew gently until quite tender.

Then rub through a hair sieve.

Whip the whites of the eggs.

When the apple pulp is quite cold, add them to it, and beat until the mixture is a stiff froth.

Colour prettily with cochineal, and heap on a glass dish.

Welsh Custard.

Ingredients—2 lb. of apples.
The thin rind of a lemon.
Juice of half a lemon.
3 oz. of castor sugar.
2 teaspoonfuls of ground ginger.
3 whole eggs.
¾ pint of water.

Method.—Wash and cut up the apples.

Stew them until tender with the sugar, lemon rind and juice, ginger, and water.

Rub them through a hair sieve (there should be about one pint of pulp if the stewing has been very gentle).

Beat the eggs, and strain them into the apple pulp.

Pour the custard into a jug.

Put it to stand in a saucepan of boiling water, and stir until it thickens, taking care that it does not curdle.

Stir occasionally while it is cooling, and serve in custard glasses or on a glass dish.

Cheap Custard.

Ingredients—1 tablespoonful of cornflour.
1 pint of milk.
The yolks of 2 eggs.
2 oz. of castor sugar.

Vanilla or other flavouring.

Method.—Put the milk and sugar on to boil.

When boiling, stir in the cornflour, which should be mixed very smoothly with a little cold milk.

Boil, stirring all the time, for ten minutes.

Then remove from the fire, and, when it has cooled a little, beat in the yolks of the eggs.

Stir again over the fire to cook the eggs, but take care they do not curdle.

Flavour to taste, and when cold pour into custard glasses.

A cheaper substitute for custard may be made by omitting the eggs.

Arrowroot Custard.

Ingredients—1 pint of milk.

1 tablespoonful of arrowroot.

2 oz. of castor sugar.

The yolks of 2 eggs.

Vanilla or other flavouring.

Method.—Boil the milk with the sugar.

When boiling, pour in the arrowroot, mixed very smoothly with a little cold milk.

Stir until it boils and thickens.

Then remove it from the fire, beat in the yolks and stir until they thicken.

Plain Trifle.

Ingredients—A little red jam.

5 sponge cakes.

1 doz. ratafias.

1 pint of milk.

The white of an egg.

3 eggs.

1 oz. of castor sugar.

Method.—Boil the milk with the sugar.

Beat the eggs, and stir the milk on to them.

Strain into a jug.

Place the jug in a saucepan of boiling water, and stir until the custard coats the spoon.

Then let it cool, stirring occasionally.

Cut the cakes in halves; spread them with jam; place them on a dish alternately with the ratafias.

Pour the custard over them, and set aside until quite cold. Decorate with the white of egg beaten stiffly.

Boiled Custard.

Ingredients—¾ pint of new milk.

Yolks of 5 eggs.

3 dessertspoonfuls of castor sugar.

A little flavouring of vanilla, lemon, or almond.

Method.—Boil the milk with the sugar.

Beat the yolks lightly.

Pour the milk (not too hot) on them, stirring all the time.

Strain the custard into a jug, which must be placed in a saucepan of boiling water.

Stir until it coats the spoon.

Great care must be taken that the custard does not curdle; it mast be stirred occasionally while cooling.

A cheaper custard may be made by substituting two whole eggs for the five yolks, or one whole egg and two yolks.

SOUFFLÉES AND OMELETS.

THE best cooks will sometimes fail in making soufflées, as their manufacture requires the very greatest care and attention. It is also necessary to be able to judge to a nicety the time they will take to cook, because, to be eaten in perfection, they should be served directly they are ready. In making a soufflée, be very careful to take *exact* measure of the different ingredients; a little too much flour, or rather too little milk, may make a great difference in the lightness of it. The flour should be the best Vienna.

Another point to be attended to is to whip up the whites of the eggs as stiffly as possible, and to mix them with the other ingredients very lightly. Bear in mind that the object in beating the whites of eggs is to introduce air into the soufflée; and it is the expansion of the air when the soufflée is cooking which makes it light. If the whites are mixed heavily with the other ingredients, the air which has been whipped into them is beaten out again; and consequently they fail to make the soufflée light. When the soufflée is firm in the middle, it is sufficiently cooked, and should be served with the greatest expedition, as it will begin to sink rapidly. An omelet soufflée, left in the oven two or three minutes over time, will be quite spoilt, and become tough and leathery.

Steamed soufflées are turned out of the tins they are cooked in, and served with a sauce poured round them.

Baked soufflées are served in the tins, which are slipped into a hot metal or silver case, or a napkin is folded round them.

Plain omelets are quickly made, and quickly spoiled. Some practice is required to make the plain omelet to perfection, as the art consists in folding the omelet just at the right moment, before the eggs used in them are too much set. The omelet should not be firm throughout, like a pancake, but should be moist and succulent in the middle. A very sharp fire is essential, and the omelet should not take more than three minutes in the making.

Steamed Soufflée.

Ingredients—1 oz. of butter.

1 oz. of flour.

¼ pint of milk.

4 eggs.

2 dessertspoonfuls of castor sugar.

Method.—Well grease a soufflée-tin with butter.

Fold a half sheet of kitchen paper in three.

Brush it over with melted butter, and fasten it round the top of the tin, letting it come nearly three inches above it.

Melt the butter in a small stewpan.

Mix in the flour smoothly.

Add the milk, and stir and cook well.

Mix in the sugar, and beat in the yolks of three of the eggs, one by one.

Add a little flavouring essence.

Beat the whites of four eggs to a stiff froth, and stir them in lightly.

Put the mixture at once into the tin.

Cover it with buttered paper, and steam carefully for half an hour.

When done, it will be firm in the middle.

Turn it quickly on to a hot dish, and serve at once, with wine sauce poured round it (*see* Sauces).

Cheese Fondu.

Ingredients—1 oz. of butter.

½ oz. of flour.

¼ pint of milk.

3 oz. of grated Parmesan cheese.

3 eggs.

A little pepper, salt, and Cayenne.

Method.—Prepare the tin as for a steamed soufflée.

Melt the butter in a small stewpan.

Mix in the flour smoothly, add the milk, and stir and cook well.

Add the seasoning, and beat in the yolks of two of the eggs.

Then mix in the grated cheese.

Beat the whites of the three eggs to a stiff froth, and stir them in lightly.

Put the mixture at once into the tin, and bake for twenty-five or thirty minutes.

When done, it will be firm in the middle.

Serve in the tin, with a napkin folded round it.

Omelet Soufflée.

Ingredients—2 yolks and 3 whites of eggs.

1 dessertspoonful of castor sugar.

A little flavouring essence.

Method.—Beat the yolks in a basin with the sugar, and add the essence.

Whip up the whites as stiffly as possible, and mix them lightly with the yolks.

Pour the mixture into a well-greased omelet-pan, and put it into a brisk oven for about three minutes, until of a pale-brown colour.

Turn it on to a hot dish.

Fold it over and serve quickly.

A Savoury Omelet Soufflée.

May be made by omitting the flavouring essence, and substituting pepper and salt for the sugar. The omelet should then be served with a rich gravy poured round it.

Cheese Ramequins.

Make a mixture as directed for Cheese Fondu. Partly fill little ramequin cases with it, and bake in a quick oven for a few minutes.

Batter for Fritters (Kromesky).

Ingredients—¼ lb. of flour.
1 tablespoonful of oiled butter or salad oil.
1 gill of tepid water.
The white of 1 egg, beaten to a stiff froth.
If for *sweet* fritters, castor sugar to taste.

Method.—Put the flour into a basin.
Make a hole in the middle, and put in the oil.
Stir smoothly, adding the water by degrees.
Beat until quite smooth.
Then add the beaten white, stirring it in lightly.

Apple Fritters.

Pare some nice apples.
Cut them into slices about a quarter of an inch thick, and stamp out the core with a round cutter.
Lay the rings in the batter, and cover them well with it.
Lift them out with a skewer, and drop them into hot fat (*see* French Frying).

When lightly browned on one side, turn them on to the other.

Drain them on kitchen paper.

Dish on a folded napkin, with castor sugar dusted over them.

A Small Savoury Omelet.

Ingredients—2 or 3 eggs.

1 dessertspoonful of finely-chopped parsley.

1 oz. of butter.

Pepper and salt.

Method.—Break the eggs into a basin.

Add to them the parsley, pepper, and salt.

Melt the butter in a small omelet-pan.

Beat the eggs very lightly, and pour them into the pan.

Shake and stir the mixture vigorously until it begins to set.

When some of the egg is set and the other still liquid, tilt the pan, and draw the egg quickly to the one side of it.

Leave it there to set for two or three seconds; then tilt the pan again and fold the omelet, quickly drawing it to the other side of the pan.

As soon as the outside is set, turn it on a hot dish and serve immediately.

To make an omelet successfully, a *very* quick fire is necessary; an omelet should not take more than three minutes to cook.

Larger omelets are made by using more eggs and butter and parsley in proportion.

Chopped cooked ham and kidney may be added to a savoury omelet; also mushrooms and shalots. The latter should be finely chopped, and fried in a little butter before they are used. A cheese omelet is made by adding grated Parmesan or other cheese to the mixture.

INVALID COOKERY.

Much attention should be paid to this branch of cookery. The recovery of many sick people depends, to a great extent, on their being able to take a proper amount of nourishment. This they will not be likely to do, unless the food is well cooked, and nicely served.

Everything, for an invalid, should be dressed plainly, and *well cooked*. Highly seasoned meat, rich gravies, sauces, puddings, &c., should be avoided. The digestive organs are weakened by illness, and should not be unduly taxed. All meals should be served punctually; carelessness in this respect has often been the cause of great exhaustion. A good nurse ought to watch her patients carefully, and never allow their strength to sink for want of nourishment at the right time.

It is not wise to prepare too large a quantity of anything at one time; an invalid's appetite is generally very variable.

All fat should be carefully removed from beef-tea and broth before they are served. This can be best done when they are cold.

Great care should be taken to make everything look as tempting as possible. The tray-cloths used, glass, silver, &c., should be spotlessly clean, and bright-looking.

Raw-beef Tea.

Ingredients—Equal quantities in weight of beef and cold water.

Method.—Scrape the beef very finely, and remove the fat.

Soak the beef in the water for about half an hour, moving it occasionally with a fork.

When the juices of the meat are drawn into the water, and it has become a deep-red colour, it is ready for use and should be strained.

This tea is better made from rump or beef steak.

Do not make too much at one time. In hot weather two ounces or a quarter of a pound of meat will be quite sufficient.

Be careful that the meat is perfectly sweet and good.

Beef Tea.

Ingredients—1 lb. of rump or beef steak.

1½ pint of cold water.

Method.—Cut the steak into small pieces, and put them into a jar with the water; tie a piece of paper over the top.

Put the jar to stand in a saucepan of boiling water for four hours.

Pour the tea from the beef, and remove the fat when cold; salt can be added to taste.

Mutton Broth.

Ingredients—1 lb. of scrag end of neck of mutton.

2 pints of water.

1 tablespoonful of rice.

Salt to taste.

Method.—Cut up the mutton, and put it into a saucepan with the water.

Simmer gently for four hours.

Then strain away from the meat, and set on one side to cool.

When quite cold carefully remove the fat, and put the broth into a clean saucepan.

Put it on the fire to boil, and, when boiling, throw in the rice, which should have been well washed.

As soon as the rice is cooked, the broth is ready.

Add salt and pepper to taste.

Clear Barley-water.

Ingredients—2 oz. of pearl barley.
A little thin lemon peel.
1 pint of boiling water.
Sugar to taste.

Method.—Wash the barley, and put it into a jug with the lemon peel.
Pour the boiling water over it, and add the sugar.
Let it stand until cold, and then strain it.

Thick Barley-water.

Ingredients—2 oz. of pearl barley.
1 quart of water.
A little thin lemon peel.
Sugar to taste.

Method.—Wash the barley, and put it into a saucepan With cold water.
Boil for ten minutes.

Then throw the water away, and wash the barley. This is to blanch it. If this were not done the barley water would have a dark-coloured, unpleasant appearance.

Put it into a saucepan, with the quart of water, and boil gently for two hours.

Sweeten to taste, and then strain it.

Rice Water.

Ingredients—2 oz. of rice.

3 pints of water.

1 inch of cinnamon.

Sugar to taste.

Method.—Wash the rice well, and throw it into three pints of boiling water, with the cinnamon.

Boil gently for two hours.

Sweeten to taste, and strain.

Apple Water.

Ingredients—2 large apples.

A little thin lemon peel.

1 pint of boiling water.

Sugar to taste.

Method.—Peel and cut up the apples.

Put them into a jug with the lemon peel and sugar.

Pour over the boiling water, and cover close until cold; then strain it.

Lemonade.

Ingredients—2 lemons.

4 lumps of sugar.

1 pint of boiling water.

Method.—Take the yellow part of the lemon peel, cut very thinly, from one of the lemons.

Then remove the skin completely from them both.

Cut them into slices, and remove the pips.

Put the sliced lemon, thin peel, and sugar, into a jug; pour over the boiling water.

Cover, until cold, and then strain.

A Cup of Arrowroot.

Ingredients—½ pint of milk.

1 dessertspoonful of arrowroot.

Castor sugar.

Method.—Put the milk into a saucepan on the fire to boil.

Mix the arrowroot very smoothly with a little cold milk; when the milk boils pour in the arrowroot, and stir until the milk has thickened.

Add sugar to taste.

For water arrowroot, substitute water for milk.

Arrowroot Pudding.

Ingredients—Cup of arrowroot, made as in foregoing recipe.

1 or 2 eggs.

A little vanilla, or other flavouring.

Method.—Beat the yolks one by one into the arrowroot, and add flavouring to taste.

Beat the whites up stiffly, and stir them in lightly.

Pour the mixture into a greased pie-dish.

Bake for a few minutes, and serve as quickly as possible.

Treacle Posset.

Ingredients—½ pint of milk.

¼ pint of treacle.

Method.—Put the milk into a saucepan on the fire to boil.

When boiling, pour in the treacle.

This will curdle the milk.

Let it boil up again, and then strain it.

White-wine Whey.

Ingredients—½ pint of milk.

1 wineglass of sherry.

Sugar to taste.

Method.—The same as in foregoing recipe. Sweeten to taste.

Orangeade.

Ingredients—2 oranges.

1 pint of boiling water.

3 lumps of sugar.

Method.—Take the rind thinly from half an orange.

Put it into a jug.

Peel the oranges, and slice them, removing the pips.

Put them into the jug.

Pour the boiling water over, add the sugar, and cover closely until cold; then strain.

Toast and Water.

Ingredients—Toasted bread.

Water.

Method.—Toast a piece of crust of bread nicely, being careful not to burn it.

Plunge it into a jug of cold water, and let it stand for thirty minutes.

Then strain the water from it.

Sago Gruel.

Ingredients—½ oz. of sago.
½ pint of water.
2 lumps of sugar.

Method.—Wash the sago, and let it soak in the water for thirty minutes.
Then simmer for about thirty minutes.
Add the sugar, and it is ready.

Prune Drink.

Ingredients—2½ oz. of prunes.
1 quart of water.
1 oz. of sugar.

Method.—Cut the prunes in two.
Boil them with the sugar in the water for one hour.
Strain, and cover until cold.

Rice Milk.

Ingredients—1 oz. of rice.
1 pint of milk.
Sugar to taste.

Method.—Wash the rice, and simmer in the milk, with the sugar, for one hour.

Tapioca milk may be made in the same way. The crushed tapioca is the best.

Suet and Milk.

Ingredients—1 pint of milk.

1 oz. of suet.

Method.—Chop the suet finely.

Tie it loosely in muslin, and simmer in the milk for three-quarters of an hour; then strain.

Invalids' Soup.

Ingredients—1 pint of beef tea.

1 oz. of crushed tapioca, semolina, or sago.

The yolks of 2 eggs.

Method.—Put the beef-tea into a saucepan on the fire.

When it boils, sprinkle in the tapioca; stir, and boil for about fifteen minutes.

Then add the yolks of the eggs; stir until they thicken, but do not let the soup boil after the yolks of the eggs are in it, as that would curdle them.

Gruel.

Ingredients—1 pint of water.

2 dessertspoonfuls of fine oatmeal.

Method.—Put the water on the fire to boil.

Mix the oatmeal smoothly with cold water.

When the water in the saucepan boils, pour in the oatmeal, and stir well until it thickens.

Then put it by the side of the fire, and stir occasionally, cooking it for *quite* half an hour.

Bran Tea.

Ingredients—3 tablespoonfuls of good bran.

1 quart of water.

1 oz. of gum arabic.

1 tablespoonful of honey.

Method.—Boil the bran in the water for ten minutes.

Dissolve the gum and honey in it, and strain it through muslin.

This is a remedy for hoarseness.

Linseed Tea.

Ingredients—4 tablespoonfuls of linseed.

1 quart of boiling water.

6 lumps of sugar.

1 lemon.

Method.—Put the linseed and sugar into a jug, with the thin rind and juice of the lemon.

Pour boiling water over.

Let it stand, and then strain.

If the tea is preferred thick, two tablespoonfuls of the linseed may be boiled in the water.

Boiled Apple-water.

Ingredients—3 good sized apples.

2 oz. of sugar.

1 quart of water.

A little thin lemon-rind.

Method.—Wash the apples, and slice them.

Put them, with the sugar and lemon rind, into the water.

Boil gently for one hour.

Then strain, and cover close until cold.

Sole for an Invalid.

Grease a baking-sheet with butter.

Lay the sole on it.

Cover with greased kitchen paper, and put it into a moderate oven for fifteen or twenty minutes, according to the size of the sole.

If properly cooked, the sole will be as white and delicate as if it had been boiled.

It may be served with or without a plain white sauce.

Whiting, plaice, smelts, &c., may be cooked in the same way.

Chicken Fillets for an Invalid.

Cut some nice little fillets from the breast of a chicken, and cook them according to the directions in preceding recipe.

Sweetbreads plainly boiled.

Soak the sweetbreads in cold water for two hours.

Then put them in boiling water for six minutes.

Soak them again in cold water for twenty minutes.

Put them into boiling water or broth, and simmer them gently for thirty minutes or more, until quite tender.

Serve with or without a plain white sauce.

Other dishes suitable for the convalescent will found under the following headings:—

    Sole à la Béchamel.
    Sole à la Maître d'Hôtel.
    Whiting Boiled.
    Boiled Chicken.
    Sweetbread à la Béchamel.
    Mutton Chop.
    Rice Pudding.
    Cornflower Pudding.
    Blancmange.
    Tapioca Pudding.
    Sago Pudding.
    Haricot Soup.
    Tapioca Soup.
    Tapioca Cream.
    Oyster Soup.

SUPPER DISHES AND SALADS.

Ox Tongue.

Put it in lukewarm water; simmer for about three hours, until very tender. A very dry tongue may take four hours' gentle simmering. If very salt or much dried, soak for twelve hours before cooking.

When tender, remove the skin and cover with glaze or fine raspings.

Galantine of Fowl.

Ingredients—1 fowl.

1½ lb. of pork.

1½ lb. of veal.

Yolks of 3 hard-boiled eggs.

2 truffles.

Method.—Bone the fowl, mince the pork and veal finely, and season with pepper and salt.

Fill the fowl with the stuffing, placing in the yolks and truffles.

Shape the fowl nicely, and fasten it securely in a cloth.

Boil it according to directions for boiling meat.

When cooked, remove the cloth and put in a clean one, fastening it as before.

Put it under pressure (not too much) until it is cold.

Remove the cloth, glaze it, and garnish with aspic jelly.

Galantine of Veal.

Breast of veal boned may be used instead of a fowl to make a galantine. Roll it round the stuffing and prepare it according to directions in preceding recipe.

Galantine of Turkey.

This may be prepared like Galantine of Fowl, using larger proportions for the stuffing.

Lobster Salad.

Ingredients—1 fine lobster.

1 lettuce.

1 endive.

3 or 4 hard-boiled eggs.

Some *mayonnaise* dressing.

If possible, some aspic jelly.

Method.—Remove the flesh from the body and claws of the lobster, and cut it in pieces.

Let the lettuce be well washed and dried.

Cut it up, and mix it with the lobster and some *mayonnaise* sauce.

Put a border of chopped aspic on a dish.

Heap the salad in the middle.

Decorate the salad with pieces of endive and hard-boiled eggs cut in quarters.

Miroton of Lobster.

Ingredients—A lobster.

1 lettuce.

A small cupful of *mayonnaise* sauce.

6 hard-boiled eggs.

If possible, some aspic jelly.

Endive.

Method.—Cut the eggs at the bottom so that they will stand upright.

Then cut them in quarters, lengthwise.

Dip the ends in a little aspic jelly, or melted gelatine, and place them close together, in the form of a large circle on a flat dish with the white part inside.

Remove the flesh from the body and claws of the lobster.

Cut up the lettuce, and mix it with the lobster and *mayonnaise*.

Heap the salad in the middle of the crown of eggs.

Decorate it with endive, and put a border of aspic jelly round it.

Chicken Salad.

Ingredients—A cold chicken.

Some celery.

A lettuce.

Endive.

Beetroot.

A small cupful of *mayonnaise* sauce.

2 or 3 hard-boiled eggs.

Method.—Remove the skin of the chicken, and cut it into dice.

Cut up the celery into half-inch lengths, taking half as much celery as chicken.

Cut up the lettuce, and mix the chicken, celery, and lettuce together with the *mayonnaise*.

Put them into a salad-bowl, or heap on a dish.

Decorate with endive, beetroot, and hard-boiled eggs.

Mayonnaise of Salmon.

Ingredients—Some cold dressed salmon.

A lettuce.

Endive.

Some hard-boiled eggs.

A small cupful of *mayonnaise* sauce.

Some chopped aspic.

Method.—Break the salmon into flakes, removing the bones.

Cut up the lettuce, and mix the salad with the *mayonnaise* sauce.

Heap it lightly on a dish.

Decorate prettily with endive, and put some hard-boiled eggs, cut into quarters, round it; also, if liked, a border of aspic jelly.

Oyster Salad.

Ingredients—1 tin of oysters.

1 crisp lettuce.

1 head of celery.

A little *mayonnaise* or salad-dressing.

Method.—Wash the lettuce, and cut it coarsely.

Wash, and cut the celery into one-inch lengths,

Trim the oysters, and mix them with the salad.

Put the mixture into a salad-bowl, and pour over the *mayonnaise* or dressing.

Celery Salad.

Ingredients—2 heads of celery.

1 beetroot.

A plain salad-dressing.

Method.—Wash the celery, and cut it into half-inch lengths.

Put them in a salad-bowl, and pour the dressing over.

Garnish with a border of beetroot.

Tomato Salad.

Ingredients—A few ripe tomatoes.

Equal quantities of oil and vinegar.

1 dessertspoonful of chopped parsley.

Pepper and salt.

Method.—Slice the tomatoes and lay them on a glass dish.

Sprinkle them with the parsley.

Mix the oil and vinegar with pepper and salt, and pour over them.

Cauliflower Salad.

Ingredients—1 boiled cauliflower.

A little *mayonnaise* or salad-dressing.

Pepper and salt.

Method.—Divide the cauliflower into tufts, and remove the green leaves.

Place them on a dish, and pour the dressing over them.

Garnish with beetroot.

Potato Salad.

Ingredients—Some boiled potatoes.

1 boiled onion.

Some plain salad-dressing.

Method.—Slice the potatoes and onion thinly.

Lay them on a dish, and pour the dressing over.

If preferred, the onion may be omitted.

Haricot Salad.

Ingredients—Some nicely cooked haricot beans.

1 teaspoonful of finely-chopped parsley.

Equal quantities of oil and vinegar.

Pepper and salt.

Method.—Lay the beans in a dish.

Sprinkle them with the parsley.

Mix the oil and vinegar with the pepper and salt, and pour over them.

Lentil Salad.

Ingredients—Some boiled lentils.

A little chopped parsley.

Equal quantities of oil and vinegar.

Pepper and salt.

Method.—Lay the lentils in a dish.

Sprinkle them with the chopped parsley.

Mix the oil and vinegar with the pepper and salt, and pour over them.

Mixed Salad.

Ingredients—Equal quantities of boiled potato, carrot, turnip, and beetroot.

Equal quantities of oil and vinegar.

Pepper and salt to taste.

Method.—Cut the vegetables into small dice.

Place them in a salad bowl.

Mix the oil and vinegar with the pepper and salt, and pour over them.

Spring Salad.

Ingredients—1 lettuce.

Some mustard and cress.

Endive.

Hard-boiled eggs.

Beetroot.

Watercress.

Some *mayonnaise* or salad-dressing.

Method.—Wash the vegetables well; put them in a draught to dry them quickly.

Then cut them rather coarsely.

Put them into a salad-bowl.

Pour over the dressing, and garnish with hard-boiled eggs and beetroot.

For a more elaborate salad, put the vegetables into a glass or silver dish, heaping them high in the centre.

Decorate with sprigs of endive, placing a large tuft at the top.

Round the base place the hard-boiled eggs, cut in quarters, alternately with slices of beetroot.

Finish off with a border of chopped aspic jelly.

MISCELLANEOUS DISHES.

Cheese Pâtés.

Ingredients—Some stale bread.

½ tablespoonful of hot water.

4 tablespoonfuls of grated cheese.

1 oz. of butter.

A few bread-crumbs.

Pepper and salt.

A little cayenne.

A few browned bread-crumbs.

The yolk of an egg.

Method.—Cut the bread in slices of one inch in thickness.

Stamp into rounds with a circular pastry-cutter; scoop out the inside, making little nests of them.

Fry in hot fat (*see* French Frying); drain them on kitchen paper.

Put them inside the oven to keep hot.

Put the butter and water into a saucepan on the fire to boil.

When boiling, stir in sufficient crumbs to make the mixture stiff.

Beat in the yolk, add pepper, salt, and cayenne; and stir in the cheese.

Pile the mixture on the cases; sprinkle a few browned crumbs over them and be careful to serve quite hot.

Welsh Rare-bit.

Ingredients—Some slices of bread about half an inch in thickness.

Some slices of cheese.

A little butter.

The yolk of an egg.

Pepper and salt.

A little cayenne.

Method.—Toast the bread and keep it quite hot.

Cut the cheese into very thin pieces.

Put it in a saucepan with the butter; pepper and salt to taste.

Stir until it has melted, then mix in the yolk.

Spread it on the toast, and brown before the fire.

Toasted Cheese.

Ingredients—Some slices of very hot toast.

Some slices of cheese.

Mustard, pepper and salt.

Method.—Toast the cheese nicely, and lay it quickly on hot toast.

Spread a little mustard thinly over it, with pepper and salt, and serve very hot.

Cheese Pudding.

Ingredients—3 oz. of bread-crumbs.

1 pint of milk.

¼ lb. of grated cheese.

3 eggs.

1 oz. of butter.

Pepper and salt.

A little cayenne.

Method.—Put the crumbs into a basin.

Boil the milk; pour it over them, and let them soak.

Then add the yolks of the three eggs, the grated cheese, and seasoning.

Beat the whites of the eggs to a stiff froth and stir them in lightly.

Pour the mixture into a greased pie-dish, and bake in a quick oven until well thrown up and brown.

Macaroni and Cheese.

Ingredients—¼ lb. of macaroni.

2 oz. of grated cheese.

½ pint of milk.

1 oz. of butter.

½ oz. of flour.

Pepper and salt.

A little cayenne.

Method.—Break the macaroni into small pieces, and boil in a quart of water for thirty minutes or more until the macaroni is tender.

Then strain away the water.

Melt the butter in a stewpan.

Mix in the flour smoothly.

Pour in the milk, stir, and boil well.

Then put in the macaroni, seasoning, and half the cheese.

Put the mixture into a greased pie-dish.

Sprinkle the remainder of the cheese over it, and bake in a quick oven until brown.

Macaroni Stewed in Milk.

Ingredients—¼ lb. of macaroni.

1 pint of milk.

Method.—Break the macaroni, and boil it in one quart of water for thirty minutes.

Then strain away the water, and pour in the milk.

Stew gently, stirring occasionally for thirty minutes.

This may be eaten with jam, sugar, treacle, stewed fruit, &c.

Macaroni Stewed in Stock.

Prepare according to directions in the preceding recipe, using stock instead of milk.

Macaroni is very good plainly boiled and served as a vegetable with roasted or stewed meat.

Savoury Rice.

Ingredients—1 onion.

2 oz. of rice.

1 pint of boilings from meat.

Pepper and salt.

Method.—Boil the onion until tender, then chop it finely.

Wash the rice, and boil it in the meat liquor with the chopped onion until tender.

Add pepper and salt to taste.

Cheese Sandwiches.

Ingredients—¼ lb. of grated cheese.

The yolks of 3 hard-boiled eggs.

4 slices of buttered bread.

1 oz. of butter.

Pepper and salt.

A little cayenne.

Method.—Beat the yolks well with the butter; add the cheese and seasoning. Spread the mixture on the two pieces of buttered bread, and place the others over.

Rice Stewed with Cheese.

Ingredients—½ lb. of rice.

2½ pints of water.

1 pint of milk.

2 oz. of grated cheese.

Pepper and salt.

Method.—Boil the rice gently in the water for half an hour, then add the milk and cheese and boil gently for half an hour more.

Stewed Normandy Pippins.

Ingredients—1 lb. of pippins.

1 quart of water.

6 oz. of lump sugar.

Method.—Soak the pippins in the water.

Then stew them with the sugar for one hour or more until quite soft.

ODDS AND ENDS.

Croutons of Bread for Soup.

Cut stale bread into small dice, fry them in a little butter, or in a large quantity of fat (*see* French Frying), a golden brown colour. Drain on kitchen paper and serve on a folded napkin.

Toasted Bread for Soup.

Cut toasted bread into small dice, put them on a baking-tin and place them in a quick oven for a few minutes. Serve on a folded napkin.

Bread-crumbs.

These are best made by rubbing stale bread through a wire sieve, or the crumb of stale bread may be dried in a slow oven and pounded for crumbs.

Browned Bread-crumbs.

These can be made from white crumbs, which should be put on a baking-tin and baked a golden brown colour in the oven; or the crusts of stale bread can be dried in a slow oven and pounded. Raspings can be used, but they should be rubbed through a wire sieve.

Browned Crumbs for Game.

Put white crumbs into a frying-pan with a little butter, and stir until they are lightly browned.

Macédoine of Vegetables.

Cut carrots and turnips into fancy shapes with a dry cutter, boil them separately, cooking the turnips five minutes and the carrots fifteen. Mix them with nicely boiled green peas and French beans. In the winter Moir's *Macédoine* of Cooked Vegetables, sold in tins, will be found very convenient.

Pickle for Meat.

Ingredients—1½ lb. of salt.

6 oz. of brown sugar.

1 oz. of saltpetre.

1 gallon of water.

Method.—Put the salt, sugar, and saltpetre into a large saucepan with the water.

Put it on the fire, bring it to the boil, and let it boil for five minutes.

It must be kept well skimmed.

Strain it into a large tub or basin.

When the pickle is quite cold, meat can be put into it.

Fried Parsley.

Choose nice green parsley, wash and dry it, and pick it from the stalk; put it into a wire spoon or basket, and fry in hot fat (*see* French Frying). It must be removed directly it is crisp or it will discolour; drain it on kitchen paper, and sprinkle it with salt. Parsley that has been frozen will turn black in frying.

Rendering down Fat.

Ingredients—4 lb. of any fat, cooked or uncooked.

Method.—Cut the fat into small pieces.

Put it into a large saucepan and cover with water.

Boil for one hour with the lid on the saucepan, that the steam may whiten the fat.

Then remove the lid, and boil steadily until the water has evaporated, and the fat melted out of the pieces.

Stir occasionally to prevent the fat sticking to the bottom of the saucepan and burning.

When the fat is ready, let it cool a little, and then strain it.

The pieces should be well pressed to squeeze out all the fat.

This fat may be used for frying, or plain cakes and pastry.

The quantity given is sufficient for French Frying.

To clarify Dripping.

Melt the dripping and pour it into cold water.

When cold, scrape off the sediment which will be found at the bottom.

To clarify Butter.

Boil the butter, and remove the curd as it rises.

HOW TO USE UP FRAGMENTS.

Scraps of Bread.

These may be used for puddings, or dried and powdered for crumbs; they can also be used to thicken soup.

Cold Potatoes.

These may be mashed and baked in a pie-dish, or made into balls and fried or baked; they may also be sliced and made into French salad, or used to thicken soup.

Scraps of Meat.

If there are not sufficient to re-cook for a made dish of any kind, put them into the stock-pot.

Fat, cooked or uncooked.

This can be cut in pieces and rendered down (*see* Rendering down Fat). It can be used for frying, plain pastry, and cakes.

Fat Skimmings from the Stock-pot.

This is excellent to fry cutlets, &c., in, and can be used instead of butter.

Dripping.

Clarify it and use it for frying, plain cakes, and pastry.

Scraps of Cheese.

Grate them, and use for Welsh rare-bit, macaroni cheese, cheese sandwiches, *pâtés*, &c.

Cold Vegetables.

If any quantity, re-warm them, or make into French salads. Any scraps can be put into the stock-pot.

Water in which Vegetables have been boiled.

Use this, if possible, for vegetable soups, as it contains to a great extent the valuable salts of the vegetables.

Boilings from Meats.

These, if not too salt, can be used to make pea, lentil, and other vegetable soups.

FORCEMEATS.

Veal Stuffing.

Ingredients—3 tablespoonfuls of bread-crumbs.

1 tablespoonful of finely-chopped suet.

1 dessertspoonful of finely-chopped parsley.

1 teaspoonful of dried and powdered thyme and marjoram.

1 egg.

Pepper and salt.

Method.—Mix all the ingredients with the egg well beaten.

A little grated lemon rind and juice improves the flavour.

Sage-and-Onion Stuffing.

Ingredients—4 onions.

¼ lb. of bread-crumbs.

7 sage leaves.

1 oz. of butter.

Pepper and salt.

Method.—Blanch the onions by putting them into cold water, and bringing it to the boil; boil for five minutes, and then throw the water away.

Rinse the onions and put them into another saucepan of water, and boil for about one hour until they are quite tender; five minutes before taking them up put in the sage leaves.

Drain the onions and sage leaves, and chop them finely; then mix them with the bread-crumbs, pepper and salt.

Quenelle Forcemeat.

See Quenelles of Veal.

Forcemeat Balls.

These are made with veal stuffing. Shape it into balls and bake them in the oven. If they are served with hare, the liver is chopped and mixed with the forcemeat.

Imitation Foie Gras.

Ingredients—½ lb. of calf's liver.
¼ lb. of bacon.
A piece of carrot, turnip, and onion.
A sprig of parsley, thyme, and marjoram.
A bay leaf.
Pepper and salt.

Method.—Slice the liver, bacon, and vegetables.

Put them into a frying-pan and cook (turning frequently) until the liver is quite tender.

Care must be taken that the liver does not fry brown.

Put the whole contents of the frying-pan into a mortar and pound well. Then rub the mixture through a hair sieve.

PRESERVES.

Strawberry Jam.

Ingredients—8 lb. of strawberries.

4 lb. of loaf sugar.

Method.—Take the stalks from the strawberries and put them in a preserving pan.

Stir and boil for thirty minutes on a moderate fire.

Then add the sugar broken into small lumps; stir and boil for about thirty minutes longer, or until the jam stiffens.

Remove all the scum as it rises.

Put the jam into pots and cover close.

Raspberry Jam.

Ingredients—6 lb. of raspberries.

3 lb. of loaf sugar.

Method.—Remove the stalks from the raspberries and boil them over a moderate fire for fifteen minutes, stirring all the time.

Add the sugar broken into lumps, and boil for about thirty minutes longer, or until the jam will set.

Remove all the scum carefully.

Put the jam into pots and cover close.

Rhubarb Jam.

Ingredients—5 lb. of rhubarb.

5 lb. of lump sugar.

Method.—Peel and cut the rhubarb as for a tart, put it in the pan with the sugar, and boil gently at first, then more quickly, skimming frequently.

When it will set it is ready.

Red Gooseberry Jam.

Ingredients—6 lb. of gooseberries.

3 lb. of lump sugar.

Water.

Method.—Take the heads and stalks from the gooseberries and put them in a pan, allowing a quarter of a pint of water to every pound of gooseberries.

Put the gooseberries into a preserving-pan.

Stir and boil for fifteen minutes.

Then add the sugar.

Continue stirring until the jam is set, skimming frequently.

Put it into pots and cover close.

Damson Jam.

Ingredients—5 lb. of damsons.

3¾ lb. of lump sugar.

Method.—Boil for thirty minutes.

Then put in the sugar broken into small pieces, and boil and skim for about twenty minutes longer, or until the jam will set.

Put into pots and cover close.

www.ingramcontent.com/pod-product-compliance
Lightning Source LLC
Chambersburg PA
CBHW081112080526
44587CB00021B/3554